THE
COMPLETE
Loran-C
HANDBOOK

LUKE MELTON

INTERNATIONAL MARINE PUBLISHING COMPANY
Camden, Maine

Published by International Marine Publishing Company

10 9 8 7 6 5 4 3

Library of Congress Cataloging in Publication Data

Melton, Luke.
  The complete Loran-C handbook.

  1. Loran.   I. Title.
VK560.M37 1986   623.89'32   86-15196
ISBN 0-87742-225-7

International Marine Publishing Company offers software for sale. For information and a catalog, please contact TAB Software Department, Blue Ridge Summit, PA 17294-0850.

Questions regarding the content of this book should be addressed to:

International Marine Publishing Company
Division of TAB Books, Inc.,
P.O. Box 220
Camden, ME 04843

Typeset by The Keyword, Inc., Belchertown, Massachusetts
Printed by Bookcrafters, Chelsea, Michigan

Contents

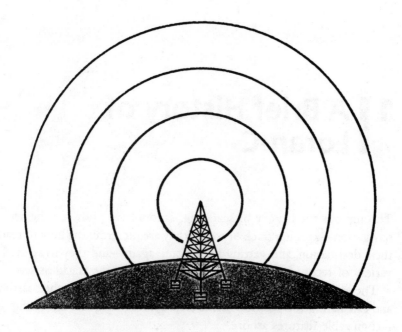

SECTION ONE

The Loran-C System

1 | A Brief History of Loran-C

Throughout the history of seafaring, sailors have practiced the art of navigation—keeping track of where they are, determining how to reach their destination, and getting back home again—and they have used a variety of techniques to guide their ships across the trackless sea.

The earliest mariners navigated by "coasting," following the coastline and calculating the position of the ship by observing its relationship to recognizable features ashore.

Driven by economic necessity, or by the desire for gold and glory, some intrepid sailors ventured farther offshore, tempting superstition and the unknown to discover what lay beyond the horizon. Living in intimate contact with the sea, these early seafarers were keen observers of the rhythms of the natural world, and they learned that the patterns of waves, the movement of celestial bodies, and the vagaries of the wind could tell them much about where they were. They were able to deduce their position by the presence of seabirds, seaweed, and sargasso, by the smells borne on the breeze, and by subtle changes in the shape and direction of waves. Their deductions were often surprisingly accurate, and many successful offshore passages to distant lands were made with little more in the way of navigational tools than a watchful eye and sensitive nose. Their deductions also were often wrong, and the reefs and shoals of the world are littered with their mistakes.

These sailors continued to push back the edges of the unknown, and slowly, painfully, their combined experiences led to the development of more accurate methods of navigation. With the invention of accurate compasses and the use of chip logs to calculate speed, navigators developed the "dead-reckoning" techniques used today; by carefully monitoring heading and speed, they could estimate the direction and distance traveled from their last known position, and thus they were able to navigate with reasonable accuracy when sailing offshore and during periods of darkness or foul weather.

As accurate sextants and chronometers became available, mariners began practicing celestial navigation, in which the varying positions of the sun, moon, and other celestial bodies, rather than terrestrial landmarks, serve as references for the calculation of a ship's position. For centuries, celestial navigation was the "state-of-the-art" technique, and even today it provides "backup" verification of positions calculated electronically. Celestial navigation represented a significant leap forward, but it had one important limitation—when celestial bodies were obscured by clouds for days on end, and on black nights when there was no horizon, a navigator was unable to take sights.

The development of radio and electronics made possible such revolutionary navigation systems as Omega, Decca, and radio direction finding (RDF), systems that enable one to calculate his position—day or night, in any kind of weather—by using electronic signals rather than geographic or celestial landmarks.

Loran, an acronym for Long-Range Navigation, is a vast improvement over all previous electronic position-finding systems. Loran-C is an all-weather, 24-hour navigation system of shore-based radio transmitting stations and shipboard radio receivers. Loran-A, the precursor of Loran-C, was developed during World War II by the Massachusetts Institute of Technology to provide the precise navigation needed for military ships and aircraft. Although rather primitive and cumbersome by today's standards, Loran-A was, nonetheless, a significant improvement over previous systems. It operated in the medium-frequency radio band of 1850–1950 kHz, had a range of only 600 nautical miles, required two large receivers, and, being sensitive to skywave effects, was frequently plagued by significant errors at night. When finally phased out late in 1980, the Loran-A system consisted of over 80 transmitting stations, many of which had been in constant use for more than 20 years.

Loran-C was developed in the late 1950s in response to the need for a new generation of radio-navigation aids. In May 1970, the Secretary of

Transportation published the *National Plan for Navigation*. This document established the Coastal Confluence Zone (CCZ)—defined as extending 50 nautical miles offshore or to the 100-fathom line, whichever is greater—and named several alternative systems of providing navigational coverage within that zone. Following extensive study, Loran-C was approved as the government-sponsored navigation system for the CCZ. Loran coverage now includes coastal areas of the contiguous 48 states, the Great Lakes, Alaska (except the North Slope), and most of the Hawaiian Islands.

Initially, Loran-C receivers were so expensive that only military ships and planes could make use of the system's benefits. Growing consumer demand, however, coupled with significant advances in the manufacture of inexpensive electronic circuits, has brought the cost of Loran-C receivers within the financial reach of most commercial and recreational boaters. As a result, with the exception of RDF, Loran-C is now the most widely used electronic coastal navigation system in the world.

2 | Theory of Operation

The land-based Loran-C radio transmitters are used in conjunction with an onboard receiver and charts "overprinted" with Loran-C lines of position. The system enables a navigator to determine his position anywhere on the sea, on land, or in the air within the coverage area.

The Loran-C system defines position in much the same way as position on the earth's surface has traditionally been defined—by creating a grid. Most navigators are quite comfortable defining their ship's position as its location on the earth's coordinate grid—that is, its latitude and longitude. When using Loran-C, position is defined in essentially the same manner, except that Loran *lines of position (LOPs)* are used (Figure 1).

As seen on a Mercator projection, parallels of latitude and meridians of longitude cross at right angles. Loran-C transmitters, on the other hand, create a grid of curved, hyperbolic lines that cross one another diagonally at various angles. As with lat/long, however, the *fix* of a ship's position is the point at which two or more Loran-C LOPs intersect.

Although the Loran system itself is very complex, the principle of operation is quite simple. One needn't be an electronics expert to use Loran-C, but a basic understanding of the system enables a navigator to use it more effectively and with greater accuracy.

Let's begin by taking a brief look at Loran-C signals using a simple analogy to illustrate the basic principle. In Figure 2, you are fishing somewhere on a large lake but are uncertain of your exact position. To the west you see a young boy standing atop a huge boulder. He throws a

5

rock into the lake, which creates a series of ripples on the water that expand outward in concentric circles from point *A*.

Seeing the rock hit the water, you decide to use the ripples to help you

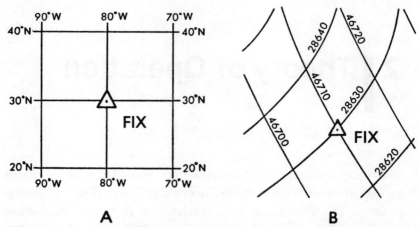

A   **B**

Figure 1 | In "A", a boat's position is defined by traditional lat/long coordinates; in "B", the same position is defined using Loran-C lines of position.

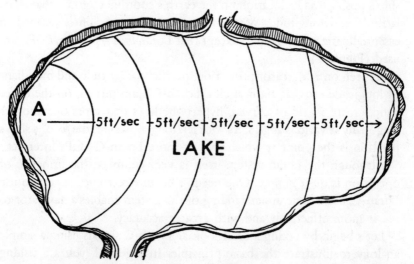

Figure 2 | Ripples travel outward from Point "A" at a velocity of 5 feet per second.

calculate your position on the lake. You reason that, if you know how fast ripples travel through water and you are able to measure the time it takes for a particular ripple to reach your boat, you can easily calculate how far your boat is from point *A*.

You remember reading somewhere that ripples have a velocity of 5 feet per second in water. Timing one specific ripple, you find that it takes 35 seconds for the ripple to reach your boat. Some simple arithmetic reveals that your boat is about 175 feet (5 times 35) from point *A*. On your map of the lake you find the symbol for the large boulder, calculate where point *A* must be, and draw a circle with a radius equal to 175 feet around it. You know that you must be somewhere on that circle—in other words, you've just plotted a circular line of position (Figure 3).

About this same time, you notice a young girl standing at the edge of the lake near an enormous pine tree. She's also chucking rocks in the water. When one of her rocks hits the water, you again start timing. It takes 20 seconds for the first ripple to reach you; you are therefore about 100 feet from point *B*. Fortunately, the pine tree the girl is standing near is so spectacularly large that its location is shown on the map of the lake.

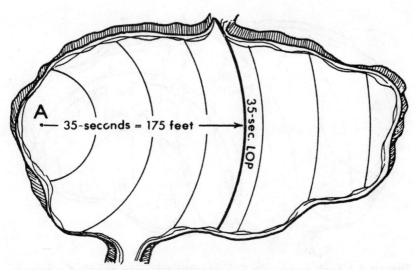

Figure 3 | At a velocity of 5 feet per second, it takes 35 seconds for the ripple to travel 175 feet.

You estimate where *B* is, draw a circle with a radius equal to 100 feet around it, and plot another LOP (Figure 4).

You now have two circular lines of position, and your boat is on both simultaneously; you therefore must be at point *X*, where they intersect.

In this rather prosaic example, you used two known facts to establish your boat's distance from two locations on the lake—the speed at which ripples travel through water, and the time required for the two ripples to arrive at your boat.

The Loran-C radio navigation system works in much the same fashion as the above illustration. Instead of rocks creating ripples in a lake, however, radio transmitters send carefully synchronized low-frequency radio signals that radiate outward (Figure 5). Given the velocity of ripples in water, the time required for the ripples to reach your boat indicated your distance from the points of impact. The velocity of radio waves in the atmosphere is known, so the time required for a radio signal to reach a receiver likewise indicates the boat's distance from the transmitter.

A Loran-C receiver, however, measures the slight interval between the *times* it receives two signals, one sent from a *master* transmitter and

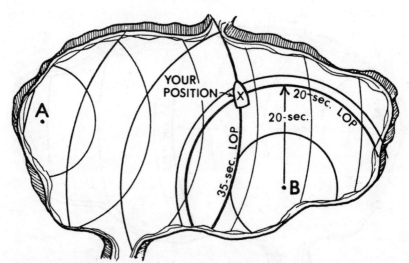

Figure 4 | Each ripple is a line of position; your position is at the point where the two LOPs intersect.

the other from one of several *secondary* transmitters. This *time difference (TD)*, which is displayed on the receiver readout, is a measure of the boat's distance from both transmitters. The boat's location, therefore, is on a line of position, the number of which is the same as the TD displayed on the receiver readout. Since a Loran receiver normally receives signals from two secondaries simultaneously, it displays two TDs as a readout on the front panel. (The TD of the master signal itself is not displayed.) The navigator then compares the TDs in the readout with the numbered lines that represent LOPs on a NOAA Loran-C overprinted chart; the lines on the chart corresponding to the numbers of the two TDs are the two LOPs on which the vessel is presently located, and the intersection of the LOPs is a fix of the boat's position.

The overprinted chart is an important element in the Loran-C system. Its use will be discussed in later chapters.

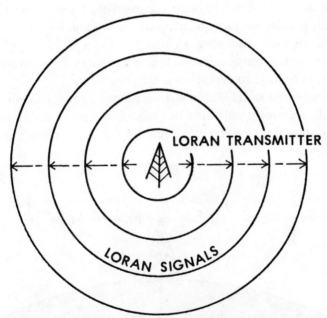

Figure 5 | Radio signals radiate outward from a Loran transmitter just as ripples travel outward from a pebble thrown in a lake.

VELOCITY OF LORAN-C SIGNALS

In the illustration of finding position on the lake, ripples traveled through the fluid medium of water at the relatively sedate velocity of 5 feet per second. Loran-C signals, on the other hand, being radio-wave transmissions, travel through the less dense medium of the atmosphere at the speed of light—186,000 statute miles per second, or 162,000 nautical miles per second. A Loran receiver is able to measure exceedingly small increments of time—as short as one-millionth of a second, which is one microsecond (1 ms). In fact, most receivers can measure even smaller fractions of time, down to one-tenth of a millionth of a second (.1 ms), and some can measure down to one-hundredth of a microsecond (.01 ms).

Even at the speed of light, the distance a radio signal travels in these very short times is likewise quite small: in 1 microsecond, a radio signal travels .162 nautical mile, or about 985 feet; in .1 microsecond, it travels one-tenth that distance, or about 98.5 feet; and in .01 microsecond, it travels about 9.85 feet. The electronic speed of a Loran-C receiver, then, makes it possible for yachtsmen to make use of radio signals as a way of establishing their positions as accurately as 100 feet—day or night, rain or shine. And, as will be discussed later, if the Loran-C system is properly used, it is realistic to expect even better accuracy.

A final word on LOPs: as was mentioned above, a Loran receiver normally receives signals from two secondary stations and displays two TDs. If, however, the receiver is receiving only one reliable secondary

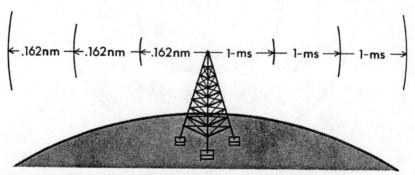

Figure 6 | For radio waves, there is a known relationship between time elapsed and distance covered.

signal at a particular time, it may still be possible to use Loran to plot a fix. If a second LOP can be obtained from some other source (such as a compass bearing to a lighthouse or buoy, or a sight on a celestial body), the single Loran LOP may then be crossed with the second LOP to provide a fix. All LOPs, regardless of their source, are lines on which your boat is located, and whenever you can get two LOPs to intersect, you've got a fix.

This, then, is the basic theory on which the Loran-C radio navigation system operates. Before discussing in detail how time differences are translated into lines of position, let's take a look at the network of Loran-C transmitting stations.

3 | Transmitter Chains

Loran-C transmitters are configured in highly synchronized chains that transmit low-frequency pulsed signals. Each chain has a master transmitter (M) and two or more secondary transmitters (W, X, Y, and Z). Transmitting stations are separated by 500 miles or more. Some chains consist of the master and only two secondary stations, whereas others contain as many as four secondaries. Most chains also include one or more *system area monitoring* (SAM) stations that monitor the transmissions of the other stations, and some chains have an experimental transmitter, usually designated TANGO, that is not used for navigation.

Each chain is designed to provide coverage for a specific geographic area, the stations being located so that transmissions from the master and at least two secondaries can be received from any location within the coverage area. There are presently 18 chains in operation worldwide, four of them in the continental United States. Although present coverage of the Northern Hemisphere is almost complete, there are still significant gaps in the Southern Hemisphere.

The U.S. chains, illustrated in Figure 7, are:

Northeast U.S. chain	GRI 9960
Great Lakes chain	GRI 8970
Southeast U.S. chain	GRI 7980
U.S. West Coast chain	GRI 9940

The Canadian East Coast chain (5930) provides coverage for the northeast coast of North America. The west coast of North America north of Seattle is covered by the Canadian West Coast chain (5990) and the Gulf of Alaska chain (7960).

Loran transmitter sites are indicated on NOAA Loran-C charts as circles, with the designation "Loran Tower." The location and specifications of Loran chains around the world can be found in *Loran-C User Handbook*, a U.S. Coast Guard publication (COMDTINST M16562.3) commonly called the "Green Book." A complete list of Loran chains can also be found in Appendix A of this book.

The Southeast U.S. (7980) chain can be used to illustrate the configuration of transmitting stations within a chain (Figure 8). This

Figure 7 | North American Loran-C transmitting chains.

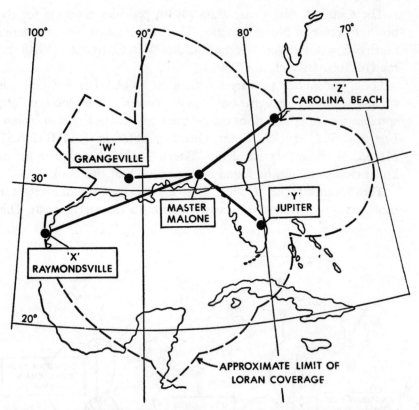

Figure 8 | The 7980 chain, which covers the southeastern United States and the entire Gulf of Mexico.

chain provides complete Loran coverage for the southeastern coast of the country, including the entire Gulf of Mexico. The master is located in Malone, Florida, near Tallahassee. The four secondaries are in Grangeville, Louisiana (W); Raymondsville, Texas (X); Jupiter, Florida (Y); and Carolina Beach, North Carolina (Z).

Incidentally, the master station and the secondary at Carolina Beach are dual-rated transmitters—they function within two chains, the 7980 Southeast U.S. chain and the 9960 Northeast U.S. chain.

4 | Group Repetition Interval

All Loran-C stations transmit on the same 100 kHz carrier frequency. If all the stations in a chain transmitted simultaneously, Loran receivers on boats within the coverage area would not be able to distinguish one station from another and therefore couldn't measure the time differences between individual transmitters. As we've seen, without the precise measurement of TDs, the Loran-C system wouldn't work. Therefore, the transmissions of each station must be timed so that signals from two stations are not received at the same time.

To prevent interference between stations, the transmissions of all stations in a chain are arranged in a precise time sequence, choreographed to ensure that the signal from one station has sufficient time to spread throughout the coverage area before the next station in the sequence transmits its signal. The unique sequencing pattern employed by each Loran chain is known as its *group repetition interval* (GRI).

First, the master station transmits a signal, which requires a certain amount of time to travel through the coverage area. The secondary in line to transmit after the master must therefore delay its transmission for a specific period, called the *secondary coding delay*. The length of this delay varies with the geographic relationship of each secondary to the master and to the other secondaries in the chain.

After the appropriate coding delay, the first secondary transmits its signal, which in turn takes time to cover the area; therefore, the next secondary must delay a certain amount of time before sending its

15

transmission. And so it goes, until all the stations in the chain have transmitted.

Each secondary station uses the master signal as a basis from which it begins timing its own unique secondary coding delay. The length of the delay is determined by a number of factors, including the length of time needed for the master signal to reach the secondary station and the propagation time needed by the previous secondary in the transmission sequence.

The master signal serves both as a timing signal and as an identifier— Loran receivers use the pulse to identify which chain's transmissions they are receiving.

To illustrate how the secondary coding delay works, let's look at the whole transmission sequence for the 7980 Southeast U.S. chain (Figure 9). Upon receiving the master pulse, each secondary in the chain begins timing its coding delay. The coding delay for the first secondary in the sequence is 11,000 microseconds; therefore, 11,000 ms after the master signal is received, the W transmitter in Grangeville transmits its signal.

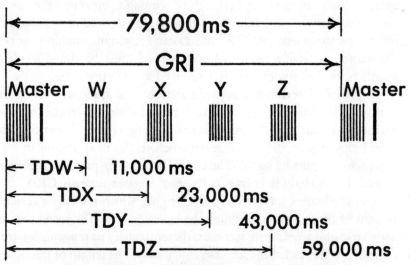

Figure 9 | Secondary stations pause for a specified time after receiving the master's signal before transmitting themselves; this is called the Secondary Coding Delay. The time between transmissions of the master is the Group Repetition Interval (GRI).

This delay is sufficient for the master signal to propagate throughout the coverage area without interference from the W signal.

The X secondary, Raymondsville, has a coding delay of 23,000 ms, so it will send its signal 23,000 ms after receiving the master signal. The coding delay for the Y secondary, in Jupiter, is 43,000 ms, and 59,000 ms after receiving the master signal, the final transmitter in the sequence, the Z transmitter in Carolina Beach, sends its signal.

Finally, 79,800 ms after its original transmission, the master transmits again. The first four digits (7980) of the interval between one transmission of the master and the next are used to identify the chain.

Each chain has a unique group repetition interval, the result of a complex interrelationship of several factors, including the speed of propagation of radio waves, the number of stations in the chain, and the distance between stations. The GRI is the minimum total time required for the master signal to reach every station in the chain, for every station to transmit, and for every transmission to propagate throughout the entire coverage area without contamination from other transmissions. And, as if that weren't complex enough, Loran GRIs, which range from 40,000 to 999,990 ms, are not only uniquely and precisely sequenced so that no signal will overlap another within the same chain, but are also designed to prevent contamination from signals transmitted in adjacent chains.

This explanation is somewhat simplified. As illustrated in Figure 9, each station actually fires multiple pulses—the master in the 7980 chain fires eight pulses 1,000 ms apart and a ninth pulse 2,000 microseconds after the eighth pulse, and each secondary fires eight pulses 1,000 ms apart. Multiple pulses contribute greatly to the enhanced reliability of Loran-C compared with Loran A.

5 | Time Differences

A Loran-C receiver is programmed to recognize the identification/timing signal sent by a master, which simultaneously establishes the chain being used and synchronizes the receiver to the master for reception of subsequent signals. Then, starting with reception of the master signal as time zero, the receiver measures the time that elapses before a signal is received from a secondary. This time difference (TD), measured in tenths of microseconds, is displayed on the receiver readout. The TD is then used to locate an LOP on a Loran-C overprinted chart and to establish a position. The receiver's ability to measure time differences precisely is critical to the success of the entire system.

In Figure 10, the master is at M and the secondary is 400 nm away, at S. The line connecting the two transmitters is the *baseline*, which is a segment of the great circle connecting the stations. When extended beyond M and S, the baseline is called the *baseline extension*. The *centerline* is perpendicular to the baseline and crosses it midway between the stations; all points on the centerline are equidistant from the master and the secondary.

In Figure 11, a boat at point A is 250 nautical miles from the master and 300 nm from the secondary. The master transmits a signal. It takes 2,470 microseconds to travel the 400 nm from the master to the secondary; but it takes only 1,543 ms for the signal to travel the 250 nm to the boat.

After receiving the master signal, the timer at the secondary station and the timer in the Loran receiver both begin timing. To avoid overlapping the master signal, the secondary must now wait through the period of its secondary coding delay, which is 15,000 ms, before

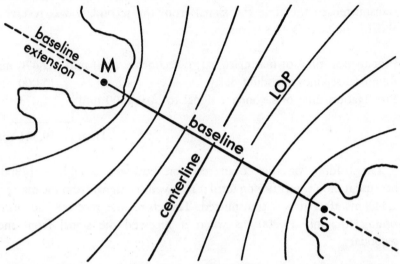

Figure 10 | The baseline, centerline, and baseline extension.

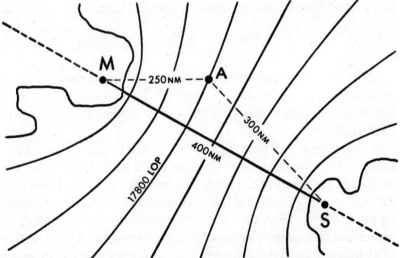

Figure 11 | Loran-C LOPs are hyperbolic curves that indicate a constant time difference in the reception of signals from the master and a secondary station.

transmitting its own signal. At the expiration of the delay time, the secondary transmits. The signal takes 1,873 ms to travel the 300 nm to the boat.

The total elapsed time from the moment the master signal was transmitted to the time the signal from the secondary was received aboard the boat is 19,343 ms.

Propagation time of master signal to secondary (400 nm)	2,470 ms
Required secondary coding delay	15,000 ms
Propagation time of secondary signal to boat (300 nm)	1,873 ms
Total	19,343 ms

The readout on the Loran receiver, however, would be 17800, because it didn't start timing until it received the signal from the master, 1,543 ms after it was transmitted. Therefore, the receiver had been timing for only 17,800 ms when it received the signal from the secondary.

Total elapsed time from transmission of the master signal to reception of secondary signal on boat	19,343 ms
Propagation time of master signal to boat (300 nm)	1,543 ms
Total time difference	17,800 ms

This 17,800 ms interval from the time the onboard Loran received the signal from the master until it received the secondary signal is the pertinent time difference (TD), and will be displayed on the receiver readout.

If one were to plot every point within the coverage area at which a Loran receiver would display this same 17800 ms TD (using the same secondary) the points would define a hyperbolic curve, or a Loran LOP. An LOP implies three useful bits of navigational knowledge: anywhere on the 17800 ms LOP, the time difference between reception of the master and secondary signals is 17,800 ms; anywhere on the 17800 ms LOP, the distance to the secondary is 50 nm farther than the distance to the master; and if the receiver displays a TD of 17800 ms, the ship is located somewhere on the 17800 ms LOP.

Because radio waves travel at a known velocity of .162 nm per microsecond, there is a direct relationship between distance and time. So, at a position that is 50 nm farther from one transmitter than it is from another, there will always be a difference of 309 microseconds in the arrival times of signals from the respective stations. Since a Loran receiver displays time difference rather than distance difference, it's easy to think only in terms of time when using Loran-C. However, a Loran LOP can be thought of as a line of both constant *time* difference and constant *distance* difference.

But why is a Loran LOP shaped like a hyperbolic curve? Doesn't this contradict an earlier statement that Loran-C signals, being radio waves, propagate outward from a transmitter in concentric circles, like ripples in a pond?

Well, radio waves *do* travel outward from the transmitter in concentric circles. If the arrival time of only one signal from one transmitter were being measured by your receiver, then the LOPs on a Loran overprinted chart would be concentric circles, and the transmitter would be at the center. The hyperbolic shape of LOPs is the result of the receiver measuring the arrival times of signals from *two different* transmitters. The LOP, therefore, is not a direct measurement of the arrival times of either of the individual signals, but a measurement of the *difference* in the times at which the two signals are received. When the distances and propagation times from two different transmitters are measured at the same time, the resulting line is neither straight nor circular—it is a hyperbolic curve.

To illustrate this point, let's look more closely at the 17800 ms displayed on the receiver's readout. In Figure 12, there are several other boats positioned along this LOP at points B, C, and D. Each boat is at a different location within the coverage area of this chain, and each is a different distance from the two transmitters than the other boats. Yet each boat's Loran receiver is displaying a TD of 17800 ms, and each is, by definition, 50 nautical miles farther from the secondary than it is from the master. If a line is drawn connecting these boats and all the other points that are 50 nm farther from the secondary than from the master the result is a hyperbolic curve—a Loran LOP. The same result could be achieved by connecting all the points at which the signal from the secondary arrives 309 ms later than the master signal, or by connecting the points at which all Loran receivers display a time difference of 17,800 ms. Every LOP is a portion of a hyperbolic curve, although on a chart they often don't appear as true hyperbolas because of chart distortion and the earth's spherical shape.

Each of the curved, colored lines on a NOAA Loran-C overprinted chart is a Loran LOP, called a *rate*. A description of the rates shown on each chart is given on the chart in a legend called the "Loran-C General Explanation" (Figure 13). This legend lists the chains covered on the chart, as well as the secondaries within each chain and the LOPs associated with each secondary.

There are, of course, almost an infinite number of possible LOPs; in order to avoid cluttering the charts with colored lines, making it difficult to read other important navigational information, only representative LOPs are shown.

The color codes used to denote the LOPs associated with each secondary are standard on all Loran-C charts:

> W – Blue
> X – Magenta
> Y – Black
> Z – Green

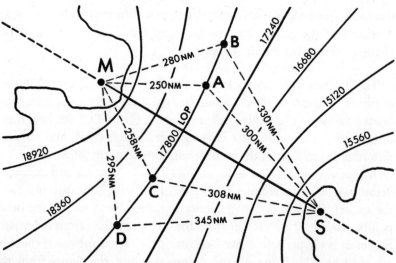

Figure 12 | Each boat on the 17800 ms LOP is 50 nm farther from the secondary transmitter than from the master.

Notice that the "General Explanation" in Figure 13 lists rates for two chains, the 7980 Southeast U.S. and the 9960 Northeast U.S. The geographic area covered by this chart, the East Coast of the United

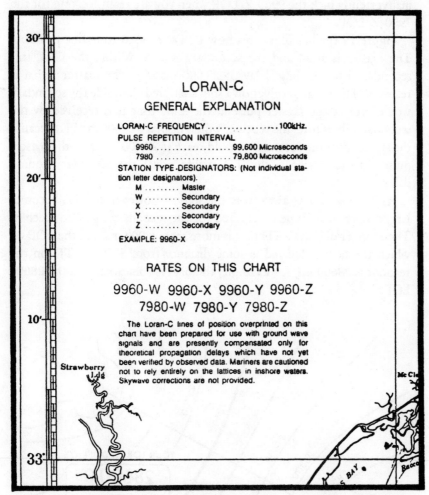

Figure 13 | The Loran-C general description and rate legend as shown on Loran-C charts. Note that LOPs for more than one chain may be printed on a single chart; here, LOPs for both the 7980 and the 9960 chains are shown. Be careful to distinguish between the W, X, Y and Z LOPs for the different chains; select the proper LOP for the chain you are using.

States around southern Georgia and northern Florida, is an area where there is overlapping coverage from these adjacent chains. Both chains have secondaries and LOPs labeled as W, Y, and Z. Be careful when reading the LOPs on this chart; since they are both green, it's easy to inadvertently pick the 9960-Z LOP when you are really looking for the 7980-Z LOP.

Figure 14 further illustrates how LOPs are used to define position. The master is at M and the secondary is at S. Within the GRI, this secondary has a coding delay of 28,000 ms after the master signal is received. The Loran receiver on a ship anchored alongside the secondary would receive the master pulse at the same time it is received by the secondary; therefore, the receiver would display a 28000 ms TD, because the signal from the secondary would reach it 28,000 ms after the master pulse. In other words, the TD would equal the secondary coding delay.

As the boat moves away from the station, however, the TD becomes larger, since more time is required for the secondary signal to reach it. The receiver displays a TD that is more than 28000 ms, and the LOP on which the boat is located is some distance from S. If the TD on the readout is 28600 ms, for example, the boat is somewhere on the 28600 LOP.

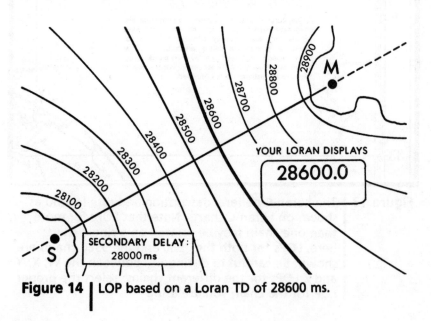

Figure 14 | LOP based on a Loran TD of 28600 ms.

Although the boat is somewhere on the 28600 LOP, this information alone is not sufficient to determine an exact location on the LOP. To get a *fix*, another LOP must be plotted. In most cases, it will be a second LOP using another secondary within the same chain. Thus, to get a fix navigating exclusively by Loran, the signals from three stations—the master and two secondaries—must be used. The receiver will display TDs of two secondaries, and these figures are used to plot the two LOPs. The point where the two LOPs intersect is a fix of the boat's present position. Loran fixes and how to plot them are discussed in Chapter 11.

This precision timing by the transmitters—the exact microseconds in the secondary coding delays and the precise measurement of time differences—is regulated by reference to an atomic clock, which uses the decay rate of the cesium atom to maintain its incredible precision. The atomic clock is accurate to within one second over 300,000 years!

6 | Technical Aspects of the Loran-C System

This chapter discusses technical aspects of the design and operation of the Loran-C system, because a more complete understanding of the technical functioning makes it possible to achieve the full accuracy that Loran-C is capable of providing.

When they were developing Loran-C, electronics engineers retained much of the basic theory of the older Loran-A. They set out, however, to make the new system more accurate, reliable, and automatic. Improvements were made in the shape and character of the transmitted signal and in the transmission format, automatic signal acquisition capabilities, and effects of skywaves. It is these changes that the system user will find most important.

TRANSMISSION FREQUENCY

The first choice engineers had to make was the radio frequency at which to transmit the Loran signal. They had a wide range of options:

VLF—Very Low Frequency (10–30 kHz). Signals propagate mainly as skywaves (discussed in detail below) or as waveguides; the reliability of such signals depends to a great extent on how accurately atmospheric conditions, primarily those in the ionosphere, are known.

LF—Low Frequency (30–300 kHz). Signals can be measured very precisely, and the effects of existing atmospheric conditions on

26

groundwaves can be predicted with considerable accuracy; long-range LF signals, however, are subject to interference from skywaves.

MF and HF—Medium and High Frequency (330–3,000 kHz). Signals can be measured accurately, but the signal strength of the groundwave is weakened considerably as the signal travels over land because of interference from natural and man-made objects whose size is a significant fraction of the signal's wavelength.

VHF—Very High Frequency (3–30 MHz). These signals and those of higher frequency are limited to "line of sight" transmissions and therefore have a very short range. A VHF marine radiotelephone is an example of a device that's severely limited in range because of operation in this frequency band.

After considering the alternatives, engineers chose the 100 kHz low-freqency band as the "carrier frequency" for Loran-C, primarily because it has relatively stable and predictable propagation characteristics and a fairly long range. Loran-C operates within the frequency band of 90 to 110 kHz.

GROUNDWAVES AND SKYWAVES

When a radio signal is transmitted, it propagates outward in all directions from the transmitter. Part of the signal travels along the curve of the earth as a *groundwave* (Figure 15). Because the groundwave follows the most direct route, the time difference between reception of the master groundwave and the reception of the secondary groundwave most accurately represents a vessel's actual distance from the transmitter. Therefore, it is the groundwave portion of a signal that should be timed by the Loran-C receiver. However, the signal strength of a groundwave is often attenuated as it follows the earth's surface because of interference from surface obstacles such as buildings, bridges, towers, etc., and the signal may be relatively weak when it finally reaches the ship. This is particularly true when operating at great distances from the transmitter, on the fringe of a coverage area.

Another part of the signal propagates upward and would continue out into space if it weren't reflected back to the earth's surface by an upper

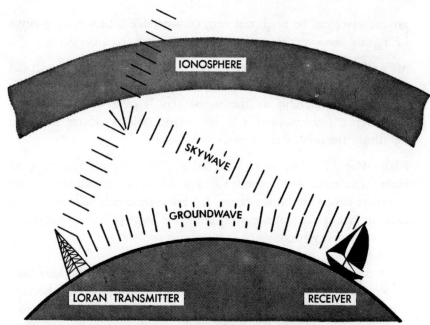

Figure 15 | Groundwaves form the part of a radio signal that travels a curved path along the earth's surface, while skywaves travel upward and are reflected back by the ionosphere. Although they travel a more direct route, groundwaves often encounter surface interference and may, therefore, produce much weaker signals than their companion skywaves.

layer of the atmosphere called the ionosphere. This reflected radio wave, called a *skywave*, travels a much greater distance to reach a Loran receiver than the companion groundwave and therefore always arrives later. Because it travels through clear air with nothing to sap its strength, however, a skywave is often much stronger than its companion groundwave. A strong skywave that arrives shortly after a weaker groundwave may overpower the weaker signal and make it difficult for your receiver to read the groundwave. This is called *skywave contamination*.

Just how much later a skywave arrives depends on several factors. The distance of the ship from the transmitter determines how far each part of the signal must ultimately travel. The speed of a groundwave diminishes with distance because of "surface friction" (interference from surface objects), so the greater the distance from the source, the more slowly it will travel.

The arrival of a skywave depends on distance and the prevailing height of the ionosphere. If the ionosphere is low, a skywave travels a shorter distance and can arrive as little as 35 microseconds after its companion groundwave; in this case, it will overlap the groundwave. If the ionosphere is high, the skywave can arrive as much as 1,000 microseconds after the groundwave, overlapping the groundwave of the succeeding pulse. In either case, the result is distortion of the Loran signal in the form of fading and changes in the shape of the pulse envelope. Large errors in plotting position can result if corrections are not made to the TDs displayed on the receiver.

The atmospheric conditions that give rise to skywaves are different from day to night and in different parts of the world. In general, the groundwave is very strong close to the transmitter, and the relatively weak skywave is automatically rejected by a receiver. However, well offshore, on the fringe of a coverage area, especially at night, the groundwave can be very weak and is easily drowned out by the stronger skywave. Under these conditions, skywave contamination may cause the receiver to display a significantly erroneous TD.

Skywave contamination of Loran signals has been a persistent problem for Loran users, particularly with Loran-A, in which reception was accomplished by visually identifying the signal on an oscilloscope. A major consideration in the engineering of the Loran-C system was to minimize skywave effects.

LORAN-C PULSE ENVELOPE AND SIGNAL CHARACTERISTICS

The designers of the Loran-C system knew that errors caused by the skywave's arriving early (35 microseconds or so after the groundwave) could be minimized if the groundwave portion of the signal had sufficient strength to override the skywave and if the receiver could read it before being contaminated by the skywave. To achieve both of these requirements, it was necessary to design the Loran-C pulse so that it was significantly different from the old Loran-A signal.

Cycle Matching

The shape of a Loran signal is called its *envelope* (Figure 16). The signal is made up of a series of sine waves or *cycles*. In Loran-A the entire shape of the envelope was visually matched on an oscilloscope and was used to identify and track an incoming signal and to measure time differences. This technique is called *envelope matching*. In Loran-C, the signal is broadcast in such a way that both the envelope *and* the individual cycles can be used to measure TDs; the receiver first makes a *coarse* match of the envelope, then a *fine* match of individual cycles within the pulse. This technique, called *cycle matching*, is one of the design features that contributes to the unparalleled accuracy of Loran-C by enabling a Loran-C receiver to receive and track signals automatically.

Loran-A signals were composed of individual cycles, but the signal was so highly compressed and the cycles so closely spaced that it was difficult for the receiver to distinguish one specific cycle within a pulse from another. To make cycle matching possible, the Loran-C pulse was lengthened to 320 microseconds, with each of the 32 cycles in the pulse lasting 10 microseconds (Figure 17). This makes it much easier for a receiver to sample an individual cycle.

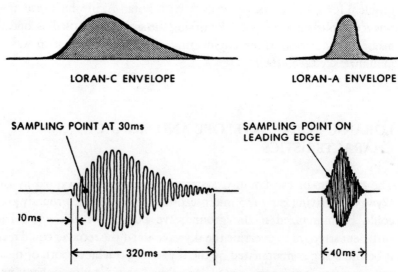

LORAN-C ENVELOPE   LORAN-A ENVELOPE

SAMPLING POINT AT 30ms   SAMPLING POINT ON
                                          LEADING EDGE

10ms

320ms   40ms

Figure 16 | Comparison of pulse and envelope shapes of Loran-A and Loran-C pulses.

Sampling

A Loran-C receiver identifies the transmitting station and measures time differences (TDs) by reading the master and secondary signals at a specific point on the pulse called the *sampling point*. The location of the sampling point is determined by the circuitry of the receiver, but it typically is on the third sine wave, 30 microseconds from the time the signal is first received (Figure 17).

Placing the point at which the signal is read on the leading edge of the pulse makes it easier for the receiver to differentiate between groundwaves and skywaves. The groundwave portion of a pulse is always received first when signals are reaching the receiver via both paths. Since skywaves can lag behind groundwaves by as little as 35 microseconds, however, the receiver must sample the groundwave's leading edge to avoid contamination in all cases. The resulting time differences accurately represent a boat's actual distance from the transmitter.

To determine the precise time difference between reception of the master and secondary signals, the receiver starts timing when it samples the 30 ms point on the master signal and stops after reading the corresponding point on the secondary pulse. This is the time interval displayed on the receiver readout as the TD.

**RAPID INCREASE IN SIGNAL
STRENGTH ON LEADING EDGE**

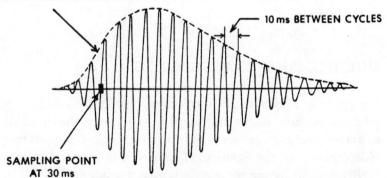

10 ms BETWEEN CYCLES

SAMPLING POINT
AT 30 ms

Figure 17 | The 320-ms pulse width, and the 30-ms sampling point, of Loran-C signals increases signal acquisition reliability.

In designing the Loran-C signal, the engineers not only expanded the pulse length but changed the envelope shape as well. Loran-A signals were symmetrical, much like a "bell curve" (Figure 16); the leading edge of the signal was relatively weak, and maximum signal strength wasn't achieved until midway through the pulse. Often, the signal wasn't sufficiently strong to stand out clearly from interference, making it difficult for a Loran operator, squinting at his oscilloscope, to distinguish the signal from background noise and contaminating skywaves.

The Loran-C signal was modified so that signal strength rises rapidly to maximum amplitude (height), reaching peak power early in the pulse, and then gradually falls to zero. Therefore, the Loran-C signal is comparatively strong when it is sampled, increasing the probability that it can be distinguished from skywave interference and background noise.

These changes in pulse shape and length enable a Loran-C receiver to identify more easily one specific cycle on the overall pulse. This is essential in the prevention of whole-cycle ambiguities in time difference measurement and allows achievement of the high degree of accuracy available in this form of pulse measurement.

A word of caution: When the signal is weak, as it often is in fringe areas, the receiver may inadvertently lock onto and sample the signal on the wrong cycle. This is called *cycle slip*. When it occurs, the TDs on the readout will indicate an erroneous position. The receiver is designed to indicate the occurence of cycle slip by displaying a *cycle-select warning*. Cycle slip and the cycle-select warning indication are discussed in detail in Chapter 10.

MULTIPLE-PULSE TRANSMISSIONS

The ability of a Loran receiver to lock onto and track a signal depends primarily on how strong the signal is. To ensure that a signal has maximum strength when it reaches a receiver, Loran-C stations transmit *multiple pulses*, thereby significantly improving the signal-to-noise ratio (SNR) without having to increase transmitter power.

Chapter 4 stated that Loran-C stations transmit groups of pulses at a specific group repetition interval, each GRI beginning with the initial timing pulse from the master, followed by sequential transmissions from each station. For purposes of Chapter 4, however, the signals sent by each station were treated as *single* pulses; in fact, each station transmits a *group* of pulses. The master transmits a pulse group consisting of eight pulses spaced 1000 microseconds apart and a ninth pulse 2000 microseconds after the eighth (Figure 18). Each secondary pulse group consists of eight pulses spaced 1000 microseconds apart. (Remember, each secondary also delays its transmission for the time specified in the secondary coding delay, so that its signal will not contaminate the signal of the previous transmitter.)

As explained earlier, a Loran-C receiver reads a signal at the 30 ms sampling point in order to prevent contamination from skywaves that arrive as soon as 35 ms after the groundwave. But what about contamination from late-arriving skywaves, those arriving as much as 1,000 ms after the groundwave? The interval of 1,000 ms between pulses within each pulse group reduces the probability of this form of skywave contamination.

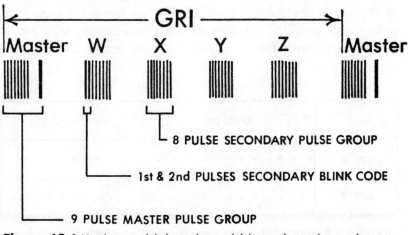

Figure 18 | Having multiple pulses within each station pulse group increases signal strength and reception reliability.

PHASE CODING

In addition to the specific timing of the multiple pulses, a technique called *phase coding*, which provides a "fingerprint" of the Loran-C signal, is used to overcome the problem of groundwave contamination from late-arriving skywaves and thereby improve the reliability of the system. Within each of the multipulse groups transmitted from the master and secondary stations, the *phase* of each pulse may be either 0 degrees "in phase" (+) or 180 degrees "out of phase" (−) with the stable 100 kHz reference signal (Figure 19). The phase code sent by a master station is different from that sent by the secondaries; all secondaries, however, send the same code. The sequence of in-phase and out-of-phase pulses is prescribed, and a Loran-C receiver is designed to search for this unique code from each category of transmitter.

For purposes of chain identification, the first group of pulses in the transmission sequence is labeled "Group A," and the second group, containing a different arrangement of + and − pulses and transmitted one GRI later, is labeled "Group B." The same A/B sequence is then repeated.

Without phase coding, contamination of a groundwave by late-arriving skywaves from the preceding signal would nullify the effect of sampling only the groundwave, thereby degrading the inherent accuracy of the system. By specifically identifying the Loran-C signal, phase coding also provides the receiver with information necessary to automatically search for the signals from the master and secondary

	MASTER	SECONDARIES
GRI 'A'	+ + − − + − + − +	+ + + + + − − +
GRI 'B'	+ − − + + + + + −	+ − + − + + − −

Figure 19 | Loran-C Phase Codes. The "A" and "B" sequences are alternated by each station. The coding is different for the master and secondaries, although all secondaries use the same code.

stations and to track them in low signal-to-noise conditions, as well as providing some protection from interference by non-Loran signals.

BLINK CODE

In the event that a secondary station's signal becomes unreliable for navigation, this fact is automatically communicated to system users by means of a *blink code*. The conditions for which a blink code would be sent are:

- TDs are out of tolerance
- Envelope-to-cycle difference (ECD) is out of tolerance
- Improper phase code or GRI
- A station is operating at less than one-half specified output power.

The blink code is initiated by reversing the polarity of the first two pulses in the secondary pulse group of the affected station or stations, and will continue until the condition is corrected. Since only the TDs of affected stations will blink, other secondaries within the chain can still be used for navigation.

In the past, the master station also transmitted a blink code, but this is no longer done. Should the master itself experience a transmission problem, your receiver will display no TDs and the entire chain will be unusable until the difficulty has been resolved. However, in some areas you may be able to switch temporarily to another chain and continue to navigate using Loran-C.

7 | Signal-to-Noise Ratio

The question is often asked, "What is the range of Loran-C coverage?" In round figures it is 1,000 to 1,200 nautical miles, but the range at which a Loran receiver aboard a vessel can reliably acquire and track a signal depends primarily on the strength of the signal (signal-to-noise ratio), the sensitivity of the receiver, and on whether or not the receiver and antenna are properly installed.

SIGNAL-TO-NOISE RATIO

The signal-to-noise ratio (SNR) is a measure of the strength of the Loran-C signal compared with the level of background noise and interference. Noise can "mask" the signal and make it difficult for the receiver to identify and continuously track it. A Loran-C user should understand signal-to-noise and how to determine the SNR of the available stations, so that he can choose the ones that will provide the most reliable reception.

To illustrate SNR, consider the operation of Loran-A: to acquire and track a signal on a Loran-A receiver, the operator had to visually match pulse envelopes on an oscilloscope and therefore had to be able to actually see the envelopes (signals) above the background radio noise. In other words, if the signal was not strong enough to stand out above the interference, he couldn't see it. If, for instance, the signal was twice as strong as the noise (the SNR was 2:1), the operator would have no

36

trouble tracking the signal. If, on the other hand, the noise was twice as strong as the signal (SNR of 1:2), the operator had to be very sharp to be able to identify and track the signal. It's worth noting that there is appreciably more background noise at 100 kHz, the Loran-C frequency, than at the old Loran-A frequencies.

Modern Loran-C receivers lock onto and track a signal automatically, but even with the wizardry of today's electronics, the receiver must still be able to distinguish the signal above the interference. Thus, the signal-to-noise ratio is still a critical factor in the reception of Loran signals. To acquire and track signals automatically, a receiver matches signals electronically (all receivers that can acquire signals automatically also track them automatically). By using the information available through cycle matching, multiple-pulse transmissions, and phase coding, receivers are able to match signals that are not strong enough to be seen above the noise (low SNR) and would be invisible on an oscilloscope. Full Loran-C coverage depends on the ability of receivers to acquire and track signals when background noise is as much as three times greater than the incoming signal, and the U.S. Coast Guard requires that all Loran-C receivers be capable of tracking signals with a minimum SNR of 1:3. With advanced circuitry, some receivers are, in fact, able to track signals with SNRs as poor as 1:10. Of course, signal strength is greater than this level in much of the Loran-C coverage area.

Thus, the "range" of Loran-C depends on the strength of the broadcast signal and the ability of a particular receiver to acquire and track a signal at that strength.

Factors affecting the SNR of signals received aboard a particular boat include distance from the transmitter, weather conditions, how the antenna was installed, whether or not the receiver is properly grounded, and the amount of interference from other electronic sources operating near the 100 kHz carrier frequency. Proper antenna installation and grounding procedures and the elimination of onboard sources of interference are discussed in Chapter 20. The elimination of external interference is covered in Chapter 10. The following paragraphs explain the effects distance and weather have on Loran-C reception and usable range.

In general, the greater the distance from a transmitting station, the weaker the signal will be, and the lower its SNR. On the fringes of an area covered by a particular Loran-C chain, even under ideal conditions, the signal will be relatively weak; a receiver may have difficulty locking onto or tracking the station. If there is a great deal of background interference, Loran use may be altogether impossible.

Weather is one of the main contributors to background noise. Cold, clear weather promotes the best Loran-C reception, and hot, moist weather the worst; thunderstorms, in particular, affect reception adversely. In fact, interference in the low-frequency radio band at which Loran-C operates comes mainly from electrical discharges in the atmosphere and from man-made sources such as electrical power generators, etc. When the weather is stormy, static can make hearing a distant AM radio broadcast difficult. The signal from a closer station, however, is strong enough to drown out the static, and reception is much better. Loran-C signals are affected in much the same way.

Unsettled weather, and especially large thunderstorms, can cause weather-related interference to be as much as four times greater than normal. Figure 20 illustrates the effects of thunderstorm activity on signal-to-noise ratio. Note that, on the graph, the range of reliable reception (indicated along the bottom) decreases about 200 nautical miles if there is a cold front between the receiver and the transmitter and 400 nautical miles if there are thunderstorms in the operating area.

The sharp decline in reliability on the left side of the graph occurs when the receiver is very close to the transmitter and the signals are too

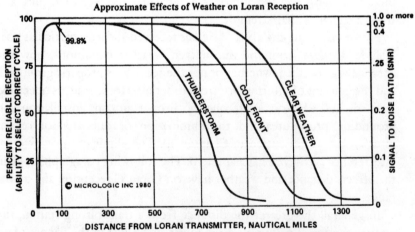

Approximate Effects of Weather on Loran Reception

Figure 20 | The effects of cold fronts and thunderstorms on Loran-C Signal-to-Noise Ratio (SNR) and range.

strong. This distortion is the result of saturating the front end of the receiver.

On the right side of the graph, the variation in signal strength is translated into signal-to-noise ratio, and the accuracy of the information displayed on the Loran-C receiver is indicated. An SNR above 0.2 indicates a reception reliability of approximately 50 percent or better, as shown on the left side of the graph; SNRs of 0.5 and over provide exceptional reliability. Notice that, even in clear weather, the SNR decreases as distance from the transmitter increases.

The percentage of reliable reception, indicated on the left side, refers to the ability of the receiver to sample the incoming signal at the intended 30-microsecond sampling point on the pulse; the lower the SNR, the greater the likelihood that the receiver will "cycle skip" and track the pulse at an incorrect point; the higher the SNR, the less likely it is that the receiver will track incorrectly.

Most present-generation Loran-C receivers will display the SNRs of the master and secondaries in a chain. Chapter 10 explains how to obtain and interpret this information.

8 | Selecting Stations

If it is used properly, the Loran-C system is capable of providing very accurate navigational information. Overall accuracy, however, depends as much on the user as on the system itself. Such factors as selecting the best secondary stations, precision in interpolating and plotting, and the proper application of required corrections will all affect ultimate accuracy. This chapter discusses selection of the most appropriate stations.

After being turned on, a receiver microprocessor will illuminate all segments of the numbers in the display as a test of the integrity of the display readout.

Most receivers automatically begin a short self-test procedure involving all internal circuits. If a discrepancy in the integrity of the operation of the receiver is detected, it will display an error or failure message. Specific error messages and their meanings are described in the operator's manual.

If the receiver indicates an internal problem during the self-test procedure, have a qualified marine electronics technician check the unit as soon as possible. If necessary, however, it may be possible to continue navigating with Loran-C despite receiver malfunctions. Although the procedure varies with the make and model of receiver, pressing the "clear" key when an error is shown will cause the receiver to bypass the error. If this procedure is followed, however, caution should be used in relying solely on the navigational information provided. If possible, use some other means to help verify the boat's position.

Most receivers automatically shut off if battery voltage drops too low, generally at about 9 volts or less. If this occurs, the computer memory will not be affected, because a built-in battery supplies reserve power to memory.

SELECTING THE CHAIN

The first step in selecting the best stations is to select the specific chain, as identified by its group repetition interval. It is preferable to use and become familiar with the chain that will answer your needs the greatest percentage of the time (in traveling from place to place, of course, it may be necessary to shift to another chain). In addition, the criteria for selecting secondaries within a chain, such as gradient, crossing angles, and proximity to baseline extensions, should influence the choice of the chain itself. These criteria are discussed in detail below.

Using the above criteria, most receivers, upon being turned on, automatically select the GRI in which the boat is currently located. In spite of this automatic acquisition feature, however, it is always a good idea to check the signal strength of the chain selected and to ensure that

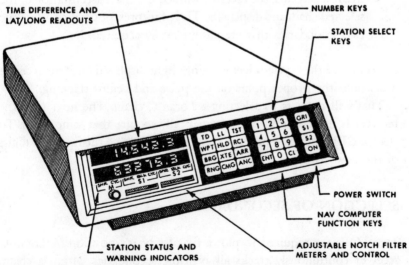

Figure 21 | Typical configuration of a Loran-C receiver.

no alarm or warning lights, such as "blink," "cycle select," or "low SNR," remain on, indicating reception problems.

Although most receivers automatically acquire the best GRI, it may be desirable to manually select a different chain. Often only one chain is available—as, for example, off the coast of Southern California or in the Gulf of Alaska. There are, however, many areas covered by two adjacent chains; charts of Loran-C coverage areas, reproduced in the Appendix, show which chains are available where. Many receivers help in making a manual selection by displaying all the chains that can be received at any time.

Once a chain is selected, its GRI will appear in the display. It is not generally necessary to renew the selection each time the receiver is turned on, because most receivers automatically acquire the most recently used chain. To select a chain the first time:

- Tell the receiver to acquire a master by pushing the GRI button

- Key in the first four digits of the desired GRI

- Verify that the numbers are correct, and execute the command by pressing the "enter" key

- In a few seconds, the receiver will acquire the master station of the selected chain and display the TDs of its present position using the two secondaries that are automatically acquired.

Expect to see the "cycle-select warning" light displayed until the receiver locks onto the proper point on the pulse and begins tracking.

That's all there is to selecting a Loran-C chain. The next time the receiver is turned on, it will automatically acquire that same chain. To change GRIs, merely repeat the above steps, entering the first four digits of the new GRI.

SELECTION OF SECONDARIES

Two LOPs are required to plot a fix of a boat's position. A Loran-C receiver continuously tracks all available secondaries within a chain, analyzes their signals, and automatically selects the two stations with the strongest and most reliable signals. The TDs of the selected pair are displayed on the readout and are the basis for all computations of the boat's present position.

In choosing the best secondaries, a receiver uses the following criteria: the *signal strength* of each secondary; the *crossing angle* between LOPs; and the *gradient* between LOPs.

Signal Strength

A significant factor in the receiver's selection of a secondary pair is the relative signal strength of the available transmitters. If all the other factors are equal, a receiver operating in the automatic station-select mode will always select the stations with the strongest signals. You can easily ascertain the signal strength of the secondaries being used by displaying the SNR of each station on the readout.

Crossing Angle

In Loran-C navigation, as in any other form of navigation, the most accurate fixes are obtained using two LOPs that cross at right angles. This ideal is seldom realized, but the selected LOPs should cross as close to 90 degrees as possible.

In practice, be wary of a fix using LOPs that cross at less than 30 degrees—at such an acute angle, the actual point of intersection becomes too ambiguous. In Figure 22, for example, the crossing angle of two of the LOPs is very shallow, and it's difficult to say for sure whether the fix is at A, B, or C.

Even more important, where LOPs cross at shallow angles, any errors made in plotting are greatly magnified compared with the same plotting error made on LOPs that cross at angles closer to 90 degrees. In Figure 23, the LOPs on the left cross at 90 degrees and intersect at one obvious point. On the right, the same LOPs are shown, but one has been accidentally misplotted a slight distance from the correct position, causing a minor shift in the point of intersection. In Figure 24, the two LOPs cross at a shallow, 25-degree angle. This results in a much less distinct point of intersection. On the right, one of the LOPs is misplotted by exactly the same amount as the misplotted LOP in Figure 23, but the position of the fix has shifted a much greater amount.

To determine the crossing angle of the LOPs from two particular secondaries, simply look on a Loran chart. Then, all other factors being

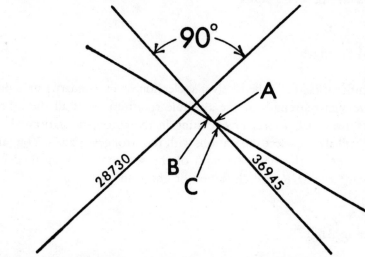

Figure 22 | For maximum accuracy, select LOPs with crossing angles as close to 90 degrees as possible.

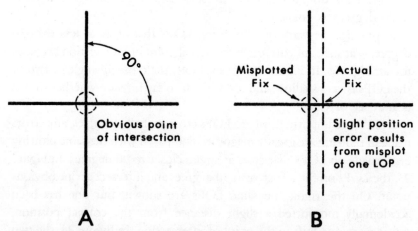

Figure 23 | LOPs crossing at 90 degrees intersect at a more distinct point; thus, plotting errors are minimized.

equal, the two stations that have the largest crossing angle should be selected. Conditions under which manual selection of secondary stations is called for are discussed later in the chapter.

Gradient

Gradient is a measure of the spacing between adjacent Loran LOPs as printed on a Loran-C overprinted chart; this spacing is measured in terms both of nautical miles and microsecond interval. Gradient is a major factor in the accuracy of positions plotted in a specific part of a coverage area; it is different at various locations within the coverage area and varies with the secondary pairs being tracked.

In Figure 25, for example, the gradient between the W LOPs of this chain is calculated based on distance (the distance between the two LOPs is 1 nautical mile) and microseconds (the interval between the LOPs is 10 ms). The overall gradient is the ratio of nautical miles to microseconds. In this illustration, 1 nm is divided by 10 ms, which means that 1 ms equals 0.1 nm, or about 608 feet. Therefore, one-tenth of a microsecond (the readout resolution on most Loran-C receivers) equals about 61 feet,

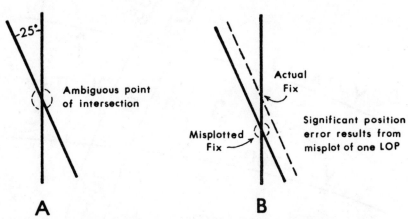

A

B

Figure 24 | When LOPs cross at angles of less than 30 degrees, not only is the point of intersection ambiguous, but any plotting errors are greatly magnified, resulting in large position errors.

and a one-tenth microsecond readout error would cause a position error of 61 feet.

Look at the gradient of the Y secondary, on the other hand. There are 3 nm between LOPs, but the microsecond interval is still 10 ms. Dividing 3 nm (18,240 feet) by 10 ms indicates that 1 ms equals 0.3 nm, or about 1824 feet. Therefore, one-tenth of a microsecond equals approximately 182 feet. Because of the greater distance separating adjacent LOPs, if the Y secondary is used, a 0.1 ms readout error causes a position error three times as large as would occur using the W LOPs! In other words, if the gradient is large, a small error in TDs on the readout will result in a large position error; if the gradient is small, the same readout error will result in a correspondingly smaller position error.

Because of the hyperbolic shape of LOPs, the gradient between adjacent ones is small near a transmitter, and increasingly larger farther from the station. For example, in Figure 26, a boat at point A is closer to

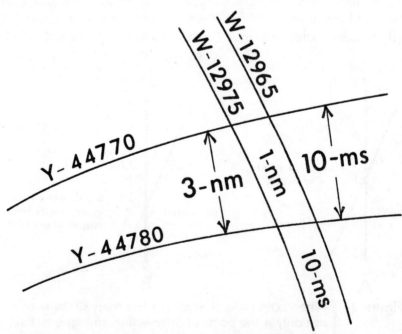

Figure 25 | The gradient between LOPs depends on the distance and the microsecond interval between them.

the W transmitter than a boat at point B, although both are exactly halfway between the W-24750 and W-24760 LOPs. Notice that the gradient at B is greater than that at A.

It is easy to determine the time difference/distance relationship for any secondary and get a good idea of the accuracy of a fix using that station. First, measure the spacing between adjacent TD lines on a Loran-C overprinted chart with dividers. Determine the distance this spacing represents in nautical miles using either the latitude scale on the sides of the chart or the graphic mileage scale. Multiply the number of nautical miles by 6,080 to convert it to an approximate number of feet. Divide the number of feet by the microsecond interval between LOPs to calculate the number of feet in one microsecond. Divide this result by 10 to determine the number of feet in one-tenth of a microsecond; this figure represents the accuracy of a Loran receiver at that geographic location using that particular secondary.

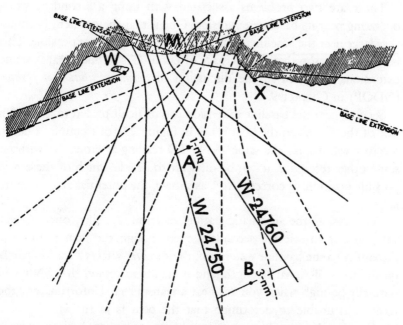

Figure 26 | Gradient is less when closer to a station, and increases as you travel farther from the station.

Distance Between LOPs	Accuracy of 0.1 ms Time Difference
1 nm	61 feet
2 nm	122 feet
3 nm	182 feet
4 nm	244 feet

PROXIMITY TO THE BASELINE EXTENSION

In manually selecting a secondary other than the ones the receiver selects automatically, choose the alternative station based on the same criteria the receiver uses, i.e., gradient, crossing angle, and signal strength. There is, however, another consideration that the receiver cannot recognize—the vessel's proximity to a *baseline extension*.

The baseline extension is the extension of a line that connects the two stations of a master/secondary pair (Figure 10). Baseline extensions of all master/secondary pairs are denoted with dashed lines and appropriately labeled on NOAA Loran-C charts.

There are two problems associated with using a secondary when operating near its baseline extension. One is that the gradient becomes very large near the baseline; thus, large position errors are possible. This is the main reason that the accuracy of Loran-C is so poor near baseline extensions, as noted in the discussion of *geometric dilution of position* (GDOP) in Chapter 9.

Second, near the baseline extension it is difficult to determine which side of the extension the boat is on. In Figure 27, for example, a Loran receiver will display the same 28490 TD reading at either X; without some other reference, it can be difficult to decide which of these two possible positions is correct. And, as shown, the potential error is quite large.

On occasion, the automatic station selection capability of a receiver will cause it to select a secondary even though the boat is in close proximity to the baseline extension; the receiver selects a station partly on the basis of signal strength, and it stands to reason that SNR will normally be high when you are near a transmitter. Unfortunately, the receiver is unable to determine that the boat is in the vicinity of a baseline extension, so it cannot reject the station on that basis. You must be aware of the fact that you are in an unreliable reception area and manually override the station selected by the receiver. Once beyond the affected area, you can switch back to the original station and take advantage of its superior signal strength.

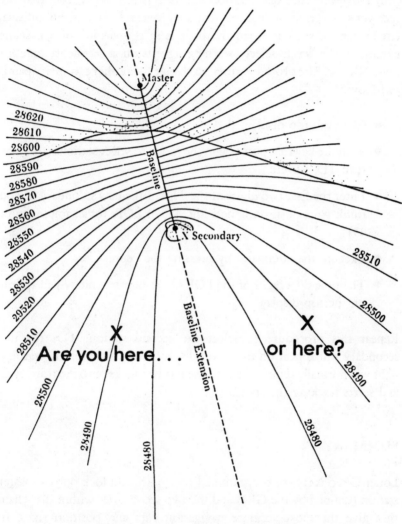

Figure 27 | Operating in the area of a baseline extension can cause position anomalies because LOPs with the same time differences can be found on both sides of the line.

MANUALLY SELECTING SECONDARIES

There are times when you may wish to switch manually to another secondary pair to cross-check or verify the position fix given by the first pair. However, automatic station selection is now so reliable that the receiver's selection should be manually overridden only in unusual circumstances, such as when the boat is in the vicinity of a baseline extension, the "cycle-select" warning light is on, a secondary exhibits low SNR, etc. The procedure used to change to another secondary pair is as follows:

- Clear the top display

- Push the key that puts you in the mode to select stations (this may read TD, S1, etc.)

- Enter the first two digits of the TDs of the new secondary (if you think your position is near the 45500 LOP, for example, enter 45)

- Execute the command by pressing the "enter" key

- The time difference of the LOP of the new secondary will appear on the top display.

Repeat this procedure to select the second station; TDs for this secondary will appear on the lower display. The "cycle-select" warning light will normally remain on until the receiver locks onto the third cycle and starts tracking the signal.

SUMMARY

Loran-C receivers are programmed to acquire and lock onto a master station (defined by the GRI) and the two secondaries within that chain that give the most accurate navigation data and position fixes. In selecting stations, the receiver analyzes the gradient between LOPs, the angle at which LOPs cross, and the strength of the incoming signals from each secondary pair.

If necessary, you can manually override both the chain and the secondary pair selected by the receiver. This should be done only when necessary, as the stations selected by the receiver are usually optimal for navigation. To ensure the most accurate fix when manually selecting stations, use the same criteria of signal strength, gradient, and crossing angle, as well as possible position ambiguities when in the vicinity of a secondary's baseline extension.

9 | Accuracy of Loran-C

One of the reasons Loran-C is so popular with the boating public is the high degree of accuracy that can be attained with the system. In fact, Loran-C can safely be said to provide accuracy greater than (or at least equal to) any other currently available navigation method. But the system isn't perfect, and to obtain the most accurate positions using Loran-C, you must be aware of its inherent limitations.

The overall accuracy of the system is affected by a number of factors, including:

- The accuracy of the transmitters
- Variability in the speeds of propagation of the transmitted signals
- Geometry of the transmitting stations
- Use of latitude/longitude conversions versus Loran-C LOPs
- Receiver quality and sensitivity
- Accuracy of Loran-C charts

Each of these contributes a degree of error, the total error depending on the magnitude of the individual errors.

In general, there are two types of accuracy: *absolute accuracy*, and *repeatable accuracy*.

ABSOLUTE ACCURACY

If you want to go to a small island in the Florida Keys but have never been there before, you might consult the NOAA Loran-C overprinted chart of the area to determine the time-difference LOPs at the location of the island. Entering these LOPs as a waypoint into the receiver's navigation computer, you follow the steering data provided by the receiver. When, according to the receiver, you've finally arrived, your distance from where you expected to be is a measure of *absolute accuracy*, often called *navigational accuracy*.

Absolute accuracy depends to a great extent on how accurately the time-difference LOPs printed on a Loran-C chart correspond to the actual latitude and longitude of a destination. When LOPs were first overprinted on charts, they were predicted using the hypothetical speed of propagation of an *ideal* signal traveling over open seawater. In reality, however, *actual* signal velocity can vary somewhat due to environmental influences encountered as the signal passes over land. As a result, the charted location of an LOP may differ to some degree from its actual location. This was a much greater problem when Loran-C first became operational. Most new charts have been corrected—the actual locations of LOPs have been determined by field verification—and most now provide a high level of accuracy.

In addition, the distance between your intended destination and the position to which your receiver leads you depends in part on the gradient between LOPs in the area. As noted earlier, gradients increase and accuracy decreases as the distance from a transmitting station increases.

Finally, absolute accuracy depends greatly on accurate measurement of the TDs of the LOP pair that define the destination; if you are careless in your chart measurements, you can expect your navigation to be in error. Chapter 11 covers the use of Loran interpolators and plotters to improve navigation accuracy.

What is the absolute accuracy of Loran-C? Under normal conditions, your position will be within about 0.1 nautical mile (500–600 feet) to 0.25 nautical mile (1,500 feet) of an intended destination to which you are navigating for the first time.

REPEATABLE ACCURACY

Repeatable accuracy is a measure of your ability to return to an exact location, the TDs of which you recorded on a previous visit. In other words, repeatable accuracy is based strictly on Loran-C LOPs, without reference to latitude/longitude coordinates.

For many Loran users, repeatable accuracy is much more important than navigational accuracy. It's often used to locate navigation aids, as, for example, finding the buoy marking the entrance to a channel when the visibility is poor. It's also used to return to a favored location. The operator of a deep-sea fishing boat, for example, might want to return to the same fishing spot, where he can be reasonably certain his charterers will catch their limit, day after day. If he can't find the right spot, his business suffers. Likewise, a dive boat operator must be able quickly and accurately to find that spectacular wreck, so that his charter divers will spread the word about how great his dive trips are.

Sometimes repeatable accuracy is used to avoid certain locations. Commercial fishermen can avoid damaging their costly nets on known snags and other underwater obstructions.

Whereas absolute accuracy can be compromised by the local variability of signal propagation, long-lived signal anomalies don't affect repeatable accuracy. You might not hit your destination right on the money the first time, but if you write down the exact time differences displayed on the receiver when you finally do find the exact spot, you can return to that spot with incredible accuracy every time. The propagation anomalies that affect a signal will have already acted on the pulse by the time a receiver picks it up. Variations in signal speed over a given land path remain fairly constant over time; therefore, each time a signal is transmitted, it will take the same amount of time to reach a given spot. So when the TDs displayed on the receiver match those you recorded, you should be within about 50 feet of your destination.

Since a high repeatable accuracy is based on the use of Loran LOPs to navigate to a destination, it follows that Loran-C time differences (LOPs) provide greater precision than the latitude/longitude readouts. Although the absolute accuracy of Loran is very good, it is in the area of "repeatability" that this navigation system excels.

ACCURACY OF THE RECEIVER

The individual receiver will affect the results obtained using the Loran-C system. The accuracy of most new receivers is quite good. However, when used in areas of poor reception, receivers with greater sensitivity will be more accurate and more reliable than those with lower sensitivity. The performance of a receiver depends very heavily on correct installation. If the receiver is improperly grounded or the antenna is mounted in a location in which incoming signal strength is weakened, the receiver will give poor performance.

The Installation chapter provides guidelines for installing the receiver and antenna, as well as for grounding the system.

THE EFFECT OF TRANSMITTER GEOMETRY ON LORAN-C ACCURACY

The configuration of the transmitters in a Loran-C chain affects the accuracy of position fixes. Within the coverage of any chain there are areas where accuracy is quite good and areas where it declines. This variability is, in part, the result of the geographic positions of the transmitters. This is called *geometric dilution of position* (GDOP) and occurs most frequently near baseline extensions and in parts of the coverage area where the LOPs have small crossing angles. In these areas, small variations in TD microsecond readings cause relatively large errors in geodetic positions.

The U.S. Coast Guard, in its book *Specifications of the Transmitted Loran-C Signal* (COMDTINST M16562.4), gives a series of Loran-C chain geometry contour charts, illustrating the expected accuracy of various combinations of master/secondary pairs. These charts map position accuracies for variations of one-tenth of a microsecond. Accuracy contours are shown for 500 feet, 1000 feet, and 1500 feet. These contour charts make it easy to select the best secondary pair to use for maximum accuracy anywhere within a coverage area, based only on GDOP. Appendix B contains reproductions of the charts for the four chains in the continental United States.

In Figure 28, accuracy contours are shown for three different combinations of master/secondary pairs in the 9940 U.S. West Coast chain: in **28A** the master at Fallon, Nevada is used along with the W secondary at George, Washington and the X transmitter at Middletown,

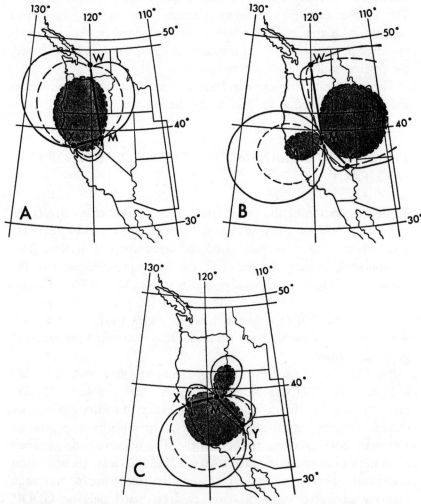

Figure 28 | Variations in accuracy caused by changes in the geometry of transmitter pairs in the U.S. West Coast chain (GRI 9940).

California. Accuracy within 500 feet is possible close to shore along a major part of the northern California and Oregon coasts; accuracy declines to 1000 feet farther west and to 1500 feet farther from the coast. Notice that accuracy declines very rapidly near the baseline extension west of Middletown.

In 28B, the master is paired with the W and Y (Searchlight) secondaries. This combination of transmitters yields accuracies of 500 feet or better only in a very restricted area around the San Francisco Bay. Accuracy declines quickly to 1000 and 1500 feet north and south of the Bay; therefore, the W/Y secondary pair should be used only on or near the San Francisco Bay. Again, note the extreme loss of accuracy near baseline extensions.

South of the San Francisco Bay (28C), accuracies of 500 feet using the X/Y secondary pair are possible only when operating close inshore along the coast.

SUMMARY

The accuracy of the Loran-C system is affected by many factors including the accuracy of the transmitters, receivers, and charts, errors in signal propagation time as a pulse travels over landmasses en route to a receiver, the geometry of transmitting stations within a chain, use of Loran TDs versus latitude/longitude coordinates to define position, and your understanding and use of the system.

Accuracy is measured in two ways: absolute, or geodetic, accuracy and repeatable accuracy. Absolute accuracy applies when you are using latitude/longitude coordinates rather than TDs to define your position, or when you obtain the time-difference coordinates of a destination directly from a NOAA chart and are navigating to that destination for the first time. Repeatable accuracy refers to how closely you can duplicate a position by matching TDs with those you obtained at that same position on a previous visit.

10 | The Loran-C Receiver

A modern Loran-C receiver is really two electronic devices—a *receiver* for acquiring and tracking signals and displaying the time differences, and a built-in *navigation computer* that computes and displays information concerning the vessel's course, speed, etc. To understand how a receiver works, it's helpful to understand the distinction between the two.

This chapter covers the Loran-C receiver. The navigational capabilities of the computer are discussed in Chapter 12.

As we have seen, the special-purpose radio receiver at the heart of a Loran unit is designed to track Loran-C radio signals and to provide the user with a readout of his position based on recorded time differences. A Loran receiver can also indicate present position in latitude/longitude coordinates.

The receiver section of a Loran-C unit also monitors a great deal of important information concerning the strength and reliability of the chain in use, the performance of the transmitters within the chain, and the operation of the receiver itself. A number of factors affect the overall performance and accuracy of the receiver, and knowing about these influences can help you use Loran-C more effectively.

BANDWIDTH

As discussed earlier, Loran-C operates in the low-frequency range of 100 kHz, and the receiver must be able to receive transmissions in that frequency range accurately and reliably. Because of differences in receivers and the way they process electronic signals, however, some models are relatively *broad-band*—they can receive signals well above and below the normal frequency range of 90–100 kHz. Others are *narrow-band* and are able to receive only signals whose frequencies are very close to the 100 kHz carrier.

There are trade-offs to both approaches. In addition to receiving the desired Loran signal, broad-band receivers may also pick up unwanted radio signals transmitted at nearby frequencies, which must then be filtered out. If the band is too narrow, on the other hand, the Loran signal may be distorted, resulting in possible TD errors, or may not be received at all if the carrier frequency wanders outside the normal range of 90–110 kHz.

SENSITIVITY

The *sensitivity* of a Loran receiver is a measure of the minimum signal strength at which the unit is able to function. This is determined by how well it receives weak signals, such as those on the fringes of a coverage area. The more sensitive a receiver, the farther from a transmitter you can operate and still rely on the accuracy of the system. In stating the sensitivity of a receiver, it is generally assumed that background interference is not excessive.

Users who expect to stay well within the normal limits of Loran-C coverage areas will find that the sensitivity of most Loran-C receivers on the market provides excellent reliability except during the most unusual weather conditions—severe thunderstorms and frequent lightning.

Users whose travels take them far offshore are often on the fringes of Loran-C coverage and may wish to purchase receivers with greater sensitivity. These units often carry a higher price tag, but having Loran aboard does little good if you are too far from a transmitter to use it. It is fair to say that, with the drop in the price of electronics in recent years, the price difference between Loran-C receivers reflects the sensitivity of the unit as well as the additional "bells and whistles" offered.

DYNAMIC RANGE

Dynamic range is the receiver's ability to process both weak and strong signals. As stated, sensitivity measures how far from a station a unit can function under low-noise conditions. Dynamic range, on the other hand, also provides a measure of how *close* to a Loran transmitter a receiver can function. A receiver with a wide dynamic range is capable of accurately processing a very strong signal from a nearby transmitter without front-end overload.

DIFFERENTIAL GAIN

Differential gain is the overall difference in strength between a master signal and a secondary signal that the receiver can accommodate. A high differential gain is desirable; the unit can successfully compare very strong signals with very weak ones, an especially important capability when operating close to a transmitting station.

READOUT RESOLUTION

Loran receivers display TDs in microseconds, tenths of microseconds, or hundredths of microseconds. The degree of *readout resolution* is very important and is a feature well worth investigating before purchasing a receiver.

As discussed in Chapter 2, a radio signal travels 0.162 nautical mile in one microsecond. If you are able to resolve propagation time to only 1 ms, the best position accuracy you can expect using Loran-C is about 985 feet; accuracy improves to about 100 feet if resolution is to 0.1 ms; and a more expensive receiver that resolves TDs to 0.01 ms can establish position within about 10 feet. If you are contemplating buying a Loran-C receiver, you'll get the high degree of accuracy Loran-C is capable of only if the receiver provides readout resolutions to at least tenths of a microsecond (Figure 29).

A somewhat less important factor regarding readouts, but one which can be very frustrating if you select the wrong kind, is *readability*. Most Loran units display TDs on a lighted panel. On older units the numbers are usually generated by light-emitting diodes (LEDs). This kind of display is fine if the receiver is installed in a relatively dark area, such as the navigation station of a large yacht. In brighter conditions, such as those found at the console of an open fishing vessel, ambient light can make it difficult if not impossible to read the display.

Most models now use liquid-crystal displays (LCDs) that generate black numbers on a light background. LCD numbers are readable in conditions that would make an LED readout impossible to see.

CYCLE-SELECT (CS) ALARM

As discussed earlier, most Loran-C receivers read a signal at the 30-microsecond sampling point on the third cycle of a pulse and track the signal automatically. The 30-ms point was chosen because it is early enough in the pulse to be ahead of any skywave contamination, yet deep enough in the pulse that the signal has time to grow strong, becoming discernible above background noise.

In a weak signal area or if there is enough interference to mask a weak signal so completely the receiver can't acquire it, the receiver may lock onto the pulse 10 ms earlier or later than the 30-ms point. This is called *cycle slip* (Figure 30). Most Loran-C receivers have automatic cycle selection and can recognize when they're tracking improperly. Under these conditions, the receiver will move up or down the pulse until it is sampling at the right spot. Until then, however, it warns of the cycle slip by activating a cycle-select (CS) alarm.

While the CS alarm is on, the receiver measures the TDs as accurately as it did before the condition occurred, but the TDs displayed are either too small or too large and will cause a position error if the LOPs are plotted. Cycle slip occurs in multiples of 10 ms, such as at the 10 ms or 50 ms points; in these cases, position errors are even greater.

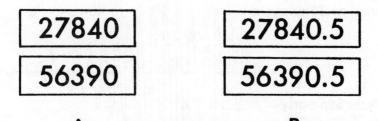

A   B

Figure 29 | The receiver "A" displays TDs to a resolution of 1 microsecond; "B" to .1 microsecond. For adequate navigational accuracy, readout resolution should be at least to .1 microsecond.

If the receiver samples a secondary pulse too early, a smaller TD will be displayed on the readout, indicating a position closer to the transmitter than is actually the case. For example, if your ship is on the 11550.0 LOP of the W secondary in the 7980 chain, the receiver should display a TD of 11550.0 (Figure 31). If, however, the receiver is sampling 10 ms too early, at the 20 ms point, the readout will show a TD of 11540.0. This would indicate that you are on an LOP that is closer to the secondary than is actually the case. If, on the other hand, the receiver samples the pulse at the 40 ms point, the readout will be 11460.0. This would indicate that you are on an LOP that is farther from the transmitter.

If cycle slip occurs on the pulse from the master station, the TDs for *both* secondaries will be wrong, and the errors in position will be *opposite* those indicated above. If the samping point is early, the position error will indicate an LOP farther from the secondary, and vice versa.

In either case, the receiver will activate the cycle-select alarm. The method chosen to indicate cycle slip varies among models and manufacturers. There is little standardization in faceplate design and the manner in which information is accessed and displayed. The operator's manual gives detailed instructions on the keystrokes used to input and output data and provides illustrations on how to interpret the readout display. Most receivers indicate any signal acquisition problem, including cycle slip, by causing the figures on the readout to flash or blink. In

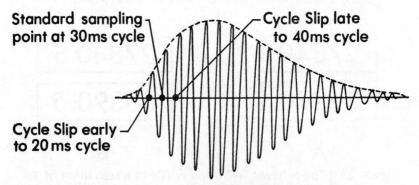

Standard sampling point at 30ms cycle

Cycle Slip late to 40ms cycle

Cycle Slip early to 20 ms cycle

Figure 30 | Cycle slip. In poor reception conditions, a receiver may inadvertently sample the point 10 ms before or after the normal sampling point on the third cycle.

general, if the numbers are flashing, assume that reception is unreliable and the stations indicated should not be used for navigation. In addition to displaying flashing numbers, many receivers pinpoint the nature of the problem more precisely; for example, CYC, SUSPECT, and CY designations are used on various receivers to warn of cycle slip. Some also have a blinking cycle-select warning light on the front panel.

CYCLE STEPPING

When operating in a fringe area, the receiver may be unable to locate the correct sampling point. In this situation, you may be able to compensate for cycle slip by using a cycle-stepping procedure, in which the TDs displayed are manually stepped up or down in 10-microsecond intervals to optimize reliability and accuracy. The procedure is relatively simple, but it should be used with caution. Before you can use cycle stepping, you must know what the TDs should be— in other words, you must already know your actual position! It is then possible to manually step the readout up or down until the correct readings are shown on the

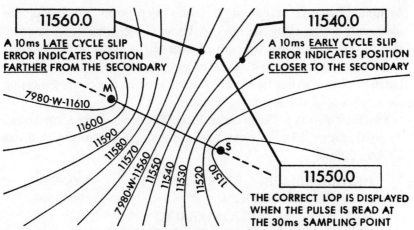

Figure 31 Your boat is actually on the 7980-W-11550.0 LOP. In "A", a 10 ms early cycle-select error places you on the 11540.0 LOP, closer to the "W" transmitter; in "B", the error is 10 ms late, placing you on the 11560.0 LOP, farther from the transmitter.

display. It is possible to cycle step the master, as well as one or both of the secondaries, if necessary. The chapter on Fringe Area Operations contains a complete discussion of cycle stepping and how it is used to improve Loran-C performance in areas of poor reception.

BLINK ALARM

If a transmission problem develops with a secondary station, the station will transmit a *blink code*, indicating that the signal is unreliable. A Loran receiver will indicate this condition by displaying a *blink alarm*. As with the cycle-select alarm, the method of indicating reception of a blink code varies: some receivers feature a light labeled "blink," but most flash the TDs of the affected secondary.

If the master station experiences out-of-tolerance conditions, your receiver will not display any stable TDs. Use another chain for navigation until the affected master is on the air again.

SNR INDICATIONS

Accurate Loran-C reception is highly dependent on having an adequately strong signal to track. A Loran-C user, therefore, must be able to check the signal strength of each of the available stations and ensure that the stations with the strongest signals are being used. Most Loran receivers can display the SNR of each station in a chain, indicating the reliability of the incoming signal.

Receivers display SNRs in coded form. The codes differ according to the particular model of receiver, but as an example, one model evaluates SNR as follows:

HIGHLY RELIABLE RECEPTION	1000–700
RELIABLE RECEPTION	700–400
MAY HAVE RECEPTION ERRORS	400–250
POOR RECEPTION, UNRELIABLE	less than 250

Some receivers display SNR in decibels (the higher numbers being the better SNRs) or as qualitative evaluations such as "very high" or "very low."

As discussed in the Installation chapter, the SNR can be used to great advantage when choosing a place to permanently mount the antenna.

Generally, the stations transmitting the strongest signals are the most reliable. But, as discussed elsewhere, signal strength is only one of several factors that should be considered in selecting the stations that will provide the best fix.

ENVELOPE TO CYCLE DISTORTION

Envelope to cycle distortion (ECD) is a measure of the distortion of Loran-C signals as they are received. ECD may be caused by several factors, such as poor antenna placement or improper installation, high levels of interference, weak signals, or the receiver being out of calibration.

The ECD of each station in a chain can be determined by going to the proper mode on the receiver. A pair of numbers will be displayed, and the difference between them indicates how much the signal from each station is distorted compared to an ideal signal.

NOTCH FILTERS

Loran-C operates on a carrier frequency of 100 kHz. Because of the nature of the pulse, the receiver must receive all transmissions in the relatively broad frequency band of 90–100 kHz. Unfortunately, this frequency band is subject to interference from a variety of external transmission sources, as well as from many common kinds of onboard equipment.

Interference causes the received pulse to be distorted and results in a loss of accuracy. If interference is strong enough, the pulse may be so badly distorted that the receiver will lock onto the wrong cycle, and if the noise level becomes much greater than the strength of the incoming signal, as can happen in extreme cases, the noise can bury the signal so completely that the receiver cannot acquire it at all, let alone accurately measure time differences.

Notch filters are designed to reduce or eliminate signal acquisition problems due to radio frequency interference from sources *external* to a vessel, such as radio broadcast stations, military radio transmitters, and other communications or navigation stations operating at frequencies near the 100 kHz band. They are not intended to filter noise generated from onboard sources, which, incidentally, often cause the greatest interference and can be the most difficult to deal with (a full discussion of onboard sources of interference is found in the Installation chapter). Although no other transmitters are allowed to operate in the Loran-C frequency band, there often is "spillover" from other transmitters. Fortunately, most of these sources of interference are well known, and interference from their transmissions can be suppressed with notch filters.

Notch filters are either the "preset frequency" type, with frequencies set at the factory or by the dealer, or the "tunable frequency" type that allow the user to select the frequencies he wants to filter out.

Most new Loran units have preset internal notch filters, the frequencies of which filter out interference within a specific, relatively narrow frequency band. They may be the proper ones to suppress typical interference for the area in which you normally operate, but there is an equal chance that they are not. Many manufacturers claim that they include the appropriate notch filters for the known sources of interference in the area to which a receiver is destined to be shipped. However, because of the wide distribution of Loran units and the sale of receivers through mail-order and discount merchandisers, it is almost impossible to know for sure that the correct filters are in your Loran when you purchase it.

There are two remedies: purchase the receiver from a marine electronics dealer who specializes in this type of equipment and who routinely tunes internal notch filters for local interference before selling a receiver, or pay a marine electronics dealer to check the filters in a receiver purchased from a discount source.

Consistently low SNRs are a good indication that the wrong notch filters have been installed in your set or that they are improperly aligned. This may occur because they weren't properly calibrated to begin with, or because, as you cruise from one section of coast to another, the external interference sources have changed. In the latter instance, you may find it necessary to take the receiver to a marine electronics technician to have the filters retuned.

Generally, if they are compatible with interference sources close to home, preset notch filters are perfectly adequate aboard vessels that remain within a specific geographic area. If, on the other hand, you plan to range widely while cruising, searching for fish, etc., you may wish to purchase a receiver with *tunable* filters, so you have greater flexibility in filtering interference throughout a wide frequency spectrum.

Receivers with tunable notch filters have an indicator (either a meter or a series of lights) that allows you to identify the interfering signal. Adjust the tuning knob until the meter indicates you are receiving the strongest signal from the interfering source, then turn the notch filter control knob until you get a minimum reading on the indicator; then, cross-check the strength of the incoming signal using the SNR mode on your receiver.

Use tunable filters cautiously, since any notching of the Loran-C signal itself will cause pulse distortion and resultant position errors. This is especially true when interference is very strong, as it may then be necessary to set the notch filters very close to the edges of the Loran-C frequency band, leaving the receiver with a very narrow bandwidth.

Some late-model receivers feature automatic notch filtering, in which the receiver determines the frequency of the noise interference and automatically adjusts the notch filters to attenuate those frequencies. Typically, there will be low-band filters (covering frequencies from about 70 kHz to 90 kHz), and two high-band filters (110 kHz to 140 kHz).

A list of the major known sources of interference and their frequencies can be found in Appendix C of this book. In most areas, strong sources of interference are not a major problem. In some, however, such as in the vicinity of Annapolis, Maryland, where the U.S. Navy has a large antenna farm transmitting at many frequencies, the interference can be so bad that Loran-C operation is not possible without proper notch filters.

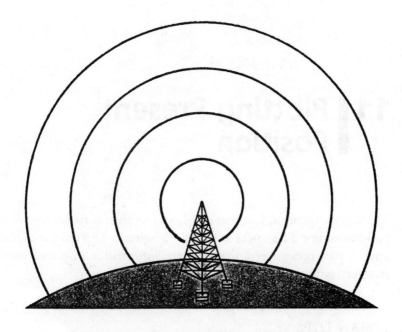

SECTION TWO

Loran
Navigation

11 | Plotting Present Position

The sole navigational function of a Loran receiver is to display present position as time differences or latitude/longitude. This chapter explains how to plot present position from the information displayed on the receiver readout.

LORAN LOPS

Let's assume that you are sailing in the Gulf of Mexico; you are using the 7980 Southeast U.S. chain and tracking the W/Z secondary pair. Your present position is displayed on the readout as:

$$
\begin{array}{ll}
\text{W} & \text{13407.6 ms TD} \\
\text{Z} & \text{58948.2 ms TD}
\end{array}
$$

To determine your present position accurately, you now must locate the LOPs that correspond exactly with these time differences on a Loran-C overprinted chart of the Gulf of Mexico.

First, a word about the chart. A Loran receiver reads out TDs to a tenth of a microsecond, so there are innumerable possible LOPs. If there were lines on the chart representing every possible LOP, the chart would be so cluttered that it would be impossible to distinguish other important information, such as the compass rose, water depths, geographic features, and navigation aids. For this reason, NOAA prints representative LOPs only, and the chart user must interpolate.

70

LOPs are printed for each secondary in a chain and are color-coded for easier identification. The same color represents the corresponding secondary on all NOAA charts, so if you are used to using the W and Y secondaries, for example, you will always look for the blue and black LOPs.

The first step in determining your present position on the chart is to find the printed LOPs that bracket each of your LOPs. Begin with the W readout (Figure 32). Your TD of 13407.6 lies between the 13400 LOP and the 13410. Then find the printed LOPs that bracket your 58948.2 LOP; your position is somewhere between the 58940 and the 58960 LOPs. To determine where your two LOPs actually are, you must learn to use a Loran-C interpolater.

An interpolator is printed somewhere on every Loran-C chart (Figure 33). It is quite easy to use once you get the hang of it. The theory behind the interpolator is illustrated thus: the 13400 and 13410 LOPs that bracket your W LOP are 10 microseconds apart, and your 13407.6 LOP is 7.6 microseconds away from the 13400. So, to find the exact place on the chart where the 13407.6 LOP lies, locate a set of points seventy-six one-hundredths of the distance between the 13400 and the 13410 LOPs.

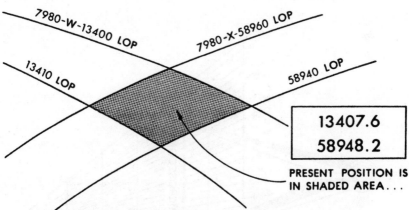

Figure 32 | With TDs of 13407.6 and 58948.2 on your Loran readout, your present position lies somewhere between the 13400 and 13410 LOPs, and the 58940 and 58960 LOPs. To determine your exact position, you must use an interpolator.

- Using a pair of dividers, measure the distance on the chart between the bracketing 13400 and 13410 LOPs.

- Retain the measured spacing and place the dividers on the interpolator so that the bottom point is on the bottom line. Holding the dividers so the legs run north and south, move the

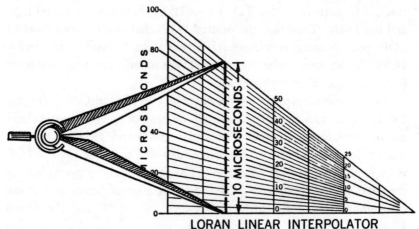

Figure 33 | A linear interpolator appears on every Loran-C over-printed chart.

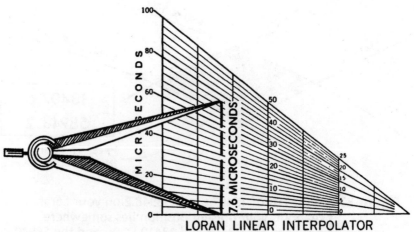

Figure 34 | Measuring a 7.6 microsecond interval on the inter-polator.

dividers east or west until the other leg falls exactly on the top line. This is the point on the interpolator that exactly matches the 10 ms spacing between the bracketing LOPs on the chart.

- Then, without moving the bottom leg, bring the top leg straight down to a point 7.6 divisions from the bottom line. (You may find it helpful to pencil in 10, 8, 6, 4, and 2 over the numbers at the left, to help you keep the numbers straight in your mind.) The space between the legs now represents 7.6 microseconds for your present needs (Figure 34).

- Place one leg of the dividers on the chart at the 13400 LOP; the other leg defines a point on the 13407.6 LOP (Figure 35).

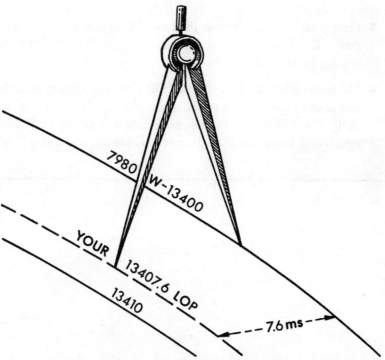

Figure 35 | Plotting the 7.6 microsecond interval measured on the interpolator. Always start from the *smaller* numbered LOP (13400) and measure towards the larger. Where the dividers fall is the point where your LOP lies, parallel to the bracketing LOPs.

- Draw a line through this point parallel to the bracketing LOPs, and you have plotted the location of your 13407.6 LOP.

If you don't have dividers handy, you can use the edge of a blank sheet of paper instead.

You can also use an interpolator issued by many Loran manufacturers. It's usually about the size of a business card, and on it are printed several scales, each of which has 10 equally spaced divisions. You can easily make one of these interpolators: simply define a space on the edge of a card or piece of paper and divide this space into 10 equal increments (Figure 36). You can make the plotter more versatile by defining spaces of varying sizes on all four sides of the card.

To use the plotter, follow these steps (Figure 37):

- Place it on the chart between the two LOPs that bracket one of your TDs. Find and use a scale on the plotter larger than the spacing between the LOPs.

- Place one end of this scale on one LOP, then *angle the card* until the line at the opposite end of the scale falls exactly on the second LOP. This divides the space between the bracketing LOPs into equal parts. In this instance, the interval between bracketing LOPs

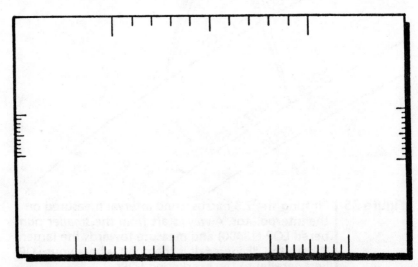

Figure 36 | A simple Loran-C plotter that you can make yourself.

is 10 microseconds, and each division on the scale equals 1 microsecond; however, the plotter can be used on any size interval between LOPs. Time difference intervals on NOAA charts may be anywhere from 2 to 50 ms, depending on the gradient at a particular location.

- Now count 7.6 increments along the scale: this distance is proportional to 7.6 microseconds out of 10 and is the spacing needed to locate the 13507.6 ms LOP.

- Draw in a line through this point parallel to the bracketing LOPs; this is your 13407.6 ms LOP.

Now, using the same technique, find the 58948.2 LOP between the 58940 and 58960 LOPs. Your fix is where the two LOPs intersect (Figure 38).

LATITUDE/LONGITUDE

A Loran receiver normally displays present position as time differences. If you wish instead to know the geodetic coordinates of your position,

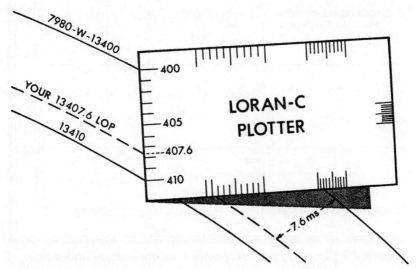

Figure 37 | Using a Loran-C plotter to establish a LOP.

the navigation computer can convert TDs to lat/long. This is generally accomplished by merely pressing the "lat/long" key on the front panel.

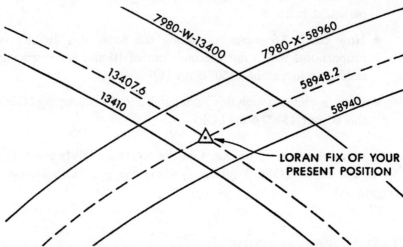

Figure 38 | Your present position is where the 13407.6 ms and the 58948.2 ms LOPs intersect.

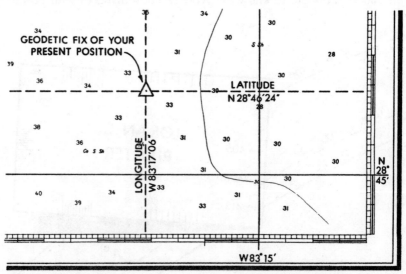

Figure 39 | Plotting present position using latitude and longitude.

On some receivers it may first be necessary to switch to the navigation mode of the computer. Normally, latitude is shown on the upper display and longitude on the lower.

Most receivers display lat/long in degrees, minutes, and *hundredths of minutes*. Lat/long coordinates on NOAA charts are graduated in degrees, minutes, and *seconds* so you must convert hundredths of minutes to seconds of arc before plotting your position. To make this conversion, multiply tenths of minutes by 60:

$$0.60 \text{ minute} \times 60 = 36 \text{ seconds}$$

$$0.80 \text{ minute} \times 60 = 48 \text{ seconds}$$

You can now use these traditional lat/long designations to plot your present position on a chart (Figure 39).

The ability of the computer to convert TDs to lat/long coordinates makes it possible to navigate effectively with Loran-C even if you don't have an overprinted chart of your operating area. The conversion to lat/long, however, introduces some degree of error into the computer position. Be sure to read the chapter on Latitude/Longitude Conversions before depending solely on this form of navigation.

12 | The Navigation Computer

Many people find technical talk rather boring, and although the receiver section is very important to the functioning of the system as a whole, the discussion of its features in Chapter 10 may have been less than exciting to you. To liven things up, let's look at the other half of the receiver, the part that has captured the popular imagination and revolutionized navigation for the average boater—the navigation computer.

The Loran-C navigation computer is a microchip built into the receiver that continually "asks" the receiver section, "What's our position?" Based on the answers the receiver supplies, the computer calculates a great deal of information about what is currently happening to the boat and predicts what will happen if conditions of heading, speed, etc. don't change.

When using a Loran unit, it's helpful to keep in mind the distinction between the navigation computer and the receiver. The receiver tracks incoming pulses and displays the measured time differences. The computer uses information provided by the receiver to calculate navigational data. If you find yourself wondering how to go about asking the unit for some piece of information, ask yourself: "Is what I want to know something that the receiver deals with, or is it navigational information that would be calculated by the computer?"

Most new Loran-C units can:

- Display present position either as TDs or as lat/long coordinates (the receiver displays position as TDs; the nav computer converts TDs to lat/long)

- Allow the user to define a variety of destinations

- Compute a course from the present position to a destination

- Tell how far it is to a destination

- Help plan a route between the present position and a final destination, particularly one that involves intermediate destinations en route

- Automatically correct for any local magnetic variation that may affect the boat's compass

- Tell what course the boat is making good, and how fast it is going

- Warn the operator if the boat strays off the intended course, tell how far off it is, and show how to get back

- Automatically steer the boat

- Use actual speed to calculate how long it will be before the boat reaches its destination

- Inform the operator that the boat is nearing its destination

- Keep watch over an anchored boat and warn if the anchor drags

- Very accurately keep track of elapsed time

In short, a Loran-C unit does just about everything. Let's take a closer look at each function of the navigation computer.

WAYPOINTS

Do you have a favorite fishing spot—maybe a great "grouper hole" where you're always sure to catch several big ones or a couple of pockets in a reef where the biggest lobsters you've ever seen set up residence? Wouldn't it be nice to be able to go back to those same spots and hit them right on the nose every time? With Loran-C, you can.

One of the most useful features of the nav computer is its ability to store and use information on geographic locations, called *waypoints*. Waypoints are places—that fishing hole, reef, or sea buoy at your homeport channel—to which your travels frequently take you.

To navigate to a waypoint, simply key its coordinates (TDs taken off a Loran-C overprinted chart or lat/long coordinates) into the computer, and it will calculate the shortest, most direct route.

If the waypoint can be reached directly, just enter its coordinates into the computer and go. Most voyages, however, whether a daysail or a week's cruise, involve changing course. Each place where the course changes becomes a waypoint; a series of related waypoints that lead to a final destination is called a *route*. Generally, you'll have more than one destination over a period of time, so waypoints are defined by numbering them sequentially. Present position is always considered to be waypoint zero (WPT 0).

Memory

The navigation computer can store a number of waypoints in *waypoint memory*: once the coordinates of a specific destination have been entered, they can be retained for later use and easily *recalled* by entering the appropriate commands into the computer. The number of waypoints that can be stored in memory varies with the make and model of the unit—some store as few as 10 waypoints, others as many as 100. If the ability to store many waypoints is important, be sure to check the capacity of waypoint memory before buying a receiver.

Many models have a convenient feature that allows the user to store the boat's present position as a waypoint; the coordinates are held in a temporary memory, to be stored in the computer's permanent memory later. Called by such names as INSTANT MEMORY, SAVE, or HOLD, this feature is useful, for example, if you pass over what seems to be a promising fishing hole or the site of a shipwreck. You want to return later to investigate, so you tell the computer to remember the coordinates. Perhaps the most important use of the SAVE feature, however, is in the event of a man overboard. Knowing the exact coordinates of the spot where the accident occurred can make it much easier to return quickly to the spot for an expeditious pickup.

On most receivers, coordinates are stored in temporary memory with a single push of the SAVE or HOLD button. The coordinates displayed on the readout at that time will be stored in temporary memory and can be retrieved later. Instant memory usually has a very limited storage capacity, and old coordinates are erased as new positions are entered.

Bearing and Range

Once the coordinates of a destination waypoint have been entered, the computer can easily compute the *bearing* and *range* (course to steer and distance) to the destination. If you have not used the local variation function of the computer (see below), the computer course to steer will be a true course. Range is normally given in nautical miles, although the computer can also display range as statute miles or kilometers if desired.

To find the bearing and range from the boat's present position to a waypoint, press the FROM–TO key (the exact wording of the key will be different on various models). This command tells the computer to calculate the bearing and range from one geographic location to another. These locations may already be defined as waypoints and stored in waypoint memory; if they aren't, enter their TDs or lat/long coordinates directly into the computer. For example, let's say you wish to know the bearing and range from your present position to the sea buoy leading into your homeport channel, the TDs of which have already been stored in the computer as WPT 1:

- Press FROM–TO
- Then, press WPT 0 (your present position)
- Then, WPT 1
- Finally, tell the computer to execute the command by pressing the ENTER key
- On the display you'll see that 064 is the true bearing from present position to WPT 1; 27.5 is the range in nautical miles.

In other words, the sea buoy at your home channel (WPT 1) bears 064 True at 27.5 nautical miles from your present position (WPT 0). If your destination isn't entered as a waypoint, simply enter its TDs or Lat/Long to get the same bearing and range information.

As the boat moves toward its destination, the bearing and range data are constantly updated. If the boat stays on the calculated course line, the bearing will not change; if it strays off course, the bearing will increase or decrease. Specific changes in bearing and range are discussed in Chapter 14.

MAGNETIC VARIATION AND DEVIATION

Courses and bearings can be displayed on Loran-C receivers as true, magnetic, or compass. Notice that the 064 bearing in Figure 40 is in degrees true. A true course must be corrected for *local magnetic variation* and *deviation* before it can be used as a steering guide.

Magnetic variation is the difference between the bearing to the geographic North Pole and the bearing to the magnetic North Pole. Variation changes as geographic position changes. The magnitude and direction (east/west) of variation is noted on NOAA charts.

Deviation is the amount by which the compass needle strays from magnetic north due to local and onboard interference. Deviation changes with changes in the boat's heading and must be determined individually for each boat.

The navigation computers in some Loran units have variation values for nearly the entire planet programmed into the microchip. These models automatically display bearings and courses as magnetic. Some models allow the user to load the deviation values for the boat into memory. Once corrected for both variation and deviation, the bearings and courses displayed by the receiver can be transferred directly to the compass.

Many receivers that don't automatically correct for variation do allow the user to input the value of local variation and will then calculate

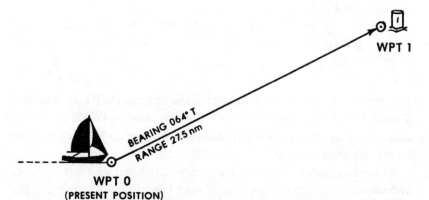

WPT 1

BEARING 064° T
RANGE 27.5 nm

WPT 0
(PRESENT POSITION)

Figure 40 | The bearing from your present position (WPT 0) to the seabuoy at your homeport channel (WPT 1) is 064 True; the range is 27.5 nautical miles.

magnetic bearings. On these models, the user must manually correct for deviation. Bear in mind that variation changes as geographic position changes. If the receiver doesn't automatically change the variation value, new values must be entered as the boat changes position.

COURSE MADE GOOD/SPEED MADE GOOD

One of the features of the navigation computer that makes it so valuable is its ability to determine what a ship is *actually* doing, instead of what it *appears* to be doing. For example, once you're on the desired heading for your destination, can you be sure that your path over the earth's surface, your *course made good* (CMG), is what you intended? Even if you've been holding the proper heading, the course you make good is often not the same at all.

And what about speed? A good knotmeter indicates very precisely speed through the water. But again, speed through the water and speed over the bottom, or speed made good (SMG), are often not the same.

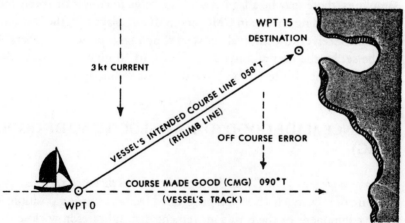

Figure 41 | Course-Made-Good (CMG) is the actual track of your boat over the bottom, as compared to the boat's DR track; Speed-Made-Good (SMG) is the boat's actual speed over the bottom, compared to indicated knotmeter speed, which is speed through the water.

Course made good and speed over the bottom have always been among the two most valuable pieces of navigational information—and the most difficult to determine (Figure 41). Current set and drift, tides, leeway, and unknown steering errors all affect the movement of a boat in subtle ways difficult to measure from onboard. They can make the direction a boat is actually heading significantly different from the compass course being steered, and the boat's speed over the surface significantly different from that shown on the knotmeter. By keeping constant track of how rapidly the boat is changing position in relation to LOPs, the navigation computer can determine velocity in relation to fixed reference points. By calculating the direction of change in position, it can calculate the course.

Course made good is indicated in degrees true, magnetic, or compass, depending on the compass corrections that have been entered into the computer. Speed made good is normally indicated in nautical miles per hours (knots). Some receivers will convert knots to statute miles per hour or kilometers per hour.

Both CMG and SMG are *averages* of the boat's course and speed over a period of time. Every three minutes or so, the computer checks the boat's present position and uses the change in position to compute a moving average. Because CMG and SMG are computed using periodic samplings, there may be a lag between a change in course or speed and the corresponding change in CMG and SMG displayed on the readout. On some receivers the interval between samplings is preset; on others, it can be set by the user and has a range of 1 to 10 minutes. Setting the interval for the shortest time gives the most stable display.

DISTANCE MADE GOOD (DMG)/VELOCITY MADE GOOD (VMG)

Distance made good (DMG), as distinguished from distance traveled, is a measure of how much a boat has progressed from its starting position; it is the component of the boat's movement that indicates how close the boat is to its destination. *Velocity made good* (VMG), as distinguished from speed over the bottom, is also a measure of progress toward a destination; it is the component of speed that indicates how much the distance from the initial starting point to the destination has been reduced over time. Both DMG and VMG refer only to the current leg of the overall route (Figure 42). In calculating DMG/VMG, the nav computer essentially disregards any sideways motion that doesn't contribute to reaching the destination.

The boat's CMG and SMG are displayed at all times, but because DMG and VMG are related to a specific destination, these variables are displayed only when there is an active destination waypoint in the computer. If progress is *toward* the destination, a "+" sign is displayed in front of the VMG readout. If the boat is heading *away* from the destination, a "–" sign is shown.

DMG and VMG are useful in optimizing progress to a destination. For example, when a sailboat is beating upwind to a mark, the effect of small changes in heading can be seen in changes in DMG and VMG. Heading up could conceivably slow the speed yet improve DMG and VMG. Falling off, on the other hand, which puts the boat on a diverging course, *could* decrease DMG and VMG while increasing SMG.

Like CMG and SMG, DMG and VMG are averages over time. When using these variables, allow time for the displayed values to catch up with

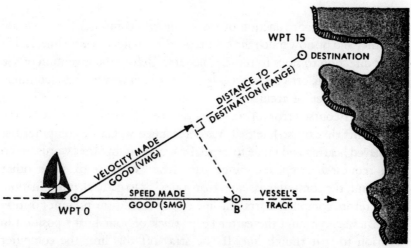

Figure 42 | Distance-Made-Good (DMG) is a measure of the progress made towards a specific destination; VMG is the speed made toward the same destination. Each applies only to the current leg of the boat's route of travel.

changes in speed or heading before analyzing their effect; 5 minutes is usually enough. DMG and VMG are displayed in the same manner as CMG and SMG.

ESTIMATED TIME EN ROUTE AND ESTIMATED TIME OF ARRIVAL

The computer uses CMG and SMG to determine how long it will take, on the current heading and at the present speed, to reach a destination (*estimated time en route* or ETE), and to forecast an *estimated time of arrival* (ETA). ETE and ETA are updated as DMG and VMG change. Because they are based on a straight line from present position to a destination, ETE and ETA are only accurate when the boat is heading directly toward that destination. ETE and ETA are displayed in the same manner as CMG, SMG, DMG, and VMG.

CROSS-TRACK ERROR

Another important function of the navigation computer is to indicate whether and by how much the boat is off the intended course line, and in what direction to steer to return to course. Before the invention of the Loran-C system, off-course error has always been very hard to determine with any degree of accuracy.

The off-course error, or *cross-track error* (XTE), indicates how far the boat is off the course line that was determined when the computer last displayed bearing and range to a specific waypoint. In other words, when you request bearing and range data from WPT 0 to some other waypoint, the computer assumes that you want to go to that destination. It therefore computes a straight-line course from your present position to that waypoint and thereafter keeps track of your boat's position in relation to that rhumb line. If you stray off this line, the computer displays the distance off course as XTE. XTE is displayed in tenths of nautical miles to the left or right of course, perpendicular to your intended track (Figure 43). Thus, you always know whether to steer to port or to starboard to return to course.

Returning to Course

There are times when you *must* remain on your original course to avoid reefs, shoals, or other hazards. In this situation, use the information provided by the XTE display to steer to port or starboard, as appropriate, to decrease the off-course error and regain your original rhumb line. To return to course in the shortest distance, turn to a heading perpendicular to the original course line.

Proceeding Directly to a Destination from an Off-Course Position

The second alternative when off course is to go directly to the destination from the boat's present position (Figure 46). The receiver will continue to indicate cross-track error. Unless you inform the computer of your intention, it will assume that you want to remain on your original rhumb line, and you will be unable to use the XTE display

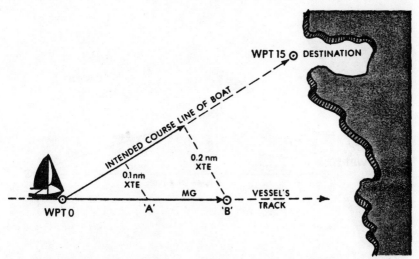

Figure 43 | Cross-Track Error (XTE). The south-setting current moves your boat south of the rhumb line between WPT 0 and WPT 15; the off-course error is displayed as XTE of .1 nm at "A", .2 nm at "B".

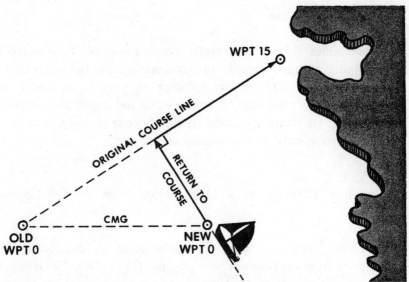

Figure 44 | When you must remain on the rhumb line to navigate safely, you can return to it most expeditiously by turning 90 degrees to the original course until XTE drops to zero.

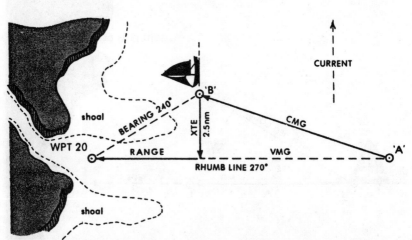

Figure 45 | In this situation, because of hazards to navigation lying between your present off-course position and your destination, it is necessary to return to the original rhumb line before proceeding to the destination.

to remain on your new course. Thus, if you decide to go directly to a destination from an off-course position, you should clear the old bearing and range data and ask the computer to recalculate navigation data from your present, off-course position.

AUTOMATIC WAYPOINT SEQUENCING

A series of waypoints can be entered into the computer (as a route, for example), and the computer will automatically sequence from one waypoint to another and provide range and bearing information for each leg of the passage. In other words, if you are operating in the *automatic waypoint sequencing* mode, when your boat arrives at the first waypoint along the route, the computer will automatically shift navigation priority to the next waypoint in the sequence and display bearing and range to that point. It will continue to sequence in this fashion until you

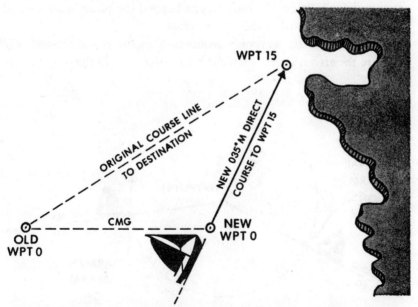

Figure 46 | If you decide to sail directly to your destination, Bearing/Range/XTE data for your new 035 Magnetic course line is obtained by clearing out the old waypoints and entering a new WPT 0 and destination.

arrive at your final destination, the last waypoint on the route. Waypoint sequencing is particularly useful when making a long passage. Waypoint sequencing and route planning are discussed more fully in Chapter 15.

ARRIVAL ALARM

When the boat is a certain distance from the destination waypoint, the computer will warn of the impending arrival by activating an arrival alarm (Figure 47). On some receivers the distance from the destination is preset (usually 0.5 nm), but many allow the user to define the radius in intervals of 0.1 nm.

In most cases, the alarm is activated as soon as the boat is within the preset radius and is deactivated when the boat travels beyond that distance on its outbound leg. Within the radius of the destination, the alarm must be shut off manually. Once turned off, the alarm won't be activated again unless the boat travels beyond the preset distance and then comes back within the alarm radius.

In the automatic waypoint sequencing mode, the computer will activate the arrival alarm when the boat arrives within the preset alarm

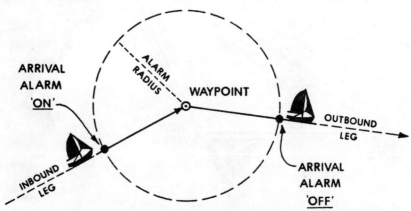

Figure 47 | The Arrival Alarm alerts the navigator to the boat's arrival within a preset radius of a destination waypoint. The alarm remains on until the boat moves beyond that radius again.

distance of each waypoint and will shut the alarm off as it switches navigation priority to the next waypoint.

The term "alarm" may be somewhat misleading—on many receivers, it's really nothing more than a beep, and usually not a very loud one, at that. You may miss it altogether if you aren't near the receiver when it comes on.

ANCHOR ALARM

A Loran unit draws little electrical power, so it can be left on when the motor is not running without fear of draining the ship's batteries. When a boat is at anchor, the receiver can be used to alert the crew if present position changes more than a preset distance from the point where the anchor was dropped—in other words, if the anchor drags.

When the anchor alarm is set, the TDs of this point are automatically stored in a separate address in waypoint memory. For this reason, you should never use the anchor alarm address to store navigation waypoints—they will be written over the next time you use the anchor alarm. To ensure that the correct TDs are stored, the anchor alarm should be set when the anchor is lowered. Selecting the anchor alarm mode on the receiver enters the TDs of the anchoring position into the

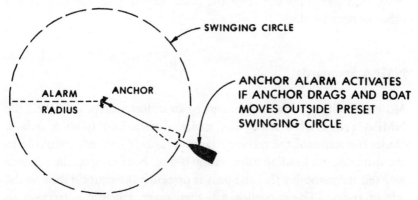

Figure 48 | The Anchor Alarm alerts the crew if the boat moves outside a circle with a preset radius; the center of the circle is the point at which the anchor is set.

computer. The radius at which the alarm will sound is preset at about 300–500 feet on some receivers; on others, it can be manually defined, generally in increments of 0.1 nm from 0.1 to 0.99 nm. This allows sufficient room for the boat to swing at anchor without tripping the alarm.

EXTERNAL ALARMS

The arrival and anchor alarms are generally indicated by a beeping sound. Unfortunately, if no one is close to the receiver, these alarms may go unnoticed. Working on the assumption that alarms are of value only if they can be heard, many manufacturers provide a way to connect the receiver to an external alarm system that produces sound loud enough to be heard from anywhere on the boat.

AUTOPILOT INTERFACE

Many Loran-C units are capable of interfacing with a ship's autopilot. Once a destination waypoint has been selected and the *autopilot interface* activated, the navigation computer will provide steering information to the autopilot that enables it to make any adjustments and corrections required to keep the boat on the desired rhumb line. Thus, the navigation computer can steer the boat, leaving you free to perform other onboard tasks.

NMEA Standards

Most autopilot interfaces conform to an industry standard called the NMEA (National Marine Electronics Association) 0180 Standard. Under this standard, the receiver transmits only cross-track error data to the autopilot; no heading information is sent. For example, the receiver may tell the autopilot that the boat is presently 0.1 nautical mile to the left of course. The autopilot will then make a gentle correction to starboard, maintaining the corrected heading until the receiver indicates that the boat is back on course, at which time it corrects back to port to resume the course line.

If the receiver's circuitry is designed to interface in conformance with another standard, the NMEA 0182 Standard, the autopilot can make use of both cross-track error and heading data. Upon reaching an intermediate waypoint along a route, the autopilot uses the bearing data supplied by the computer to turn the boat to the next heading. The autopilot then monitors cross-track error input from the computer to keep the boat near the rhumb line.

If you wish to make full use of the automatic steering capabilities available in the automatic waypoint sequencing mode, you must have a receiver capable of using the NMEA 0182 format: the computer will not only steer your vessel to a destination, but can turn the boat to the heading for the next waypoint as well. With a receiver that conforms to the NMEA 0180 standard, you must turn the vessel to the new heading yourself.

Although the receiver is capable of monitoring and displaying greater values for XTE, under NMEA standards the maximum cross-track error the computer can output to the autopilot is 0.31 nautical mile.

Using the Autopilot Interface

The boat should be on the course line to your next waypoint *before* you engage the autopilot. If you engage the autopilot before getting the boat on course and heading, one of two things can happen: the boat will make giant S turns to either side of the intended course line, or the boat will turn in circles and never cross the course line.

Making S turns is more probable. Here's how it can happen: You are 0.4 nm off course to port when you engage the autopilot (Figure 49). The computer then tells the autopilot the boat is off course to port, and the autopilot immediately responds by turning the boat to starboard. Because the boat is a considerable distance off the rhumb line, the computer continues to report the port XTE error for some time, and the autopilot continues to respond by turning starboard.

Eventually, however, the boat crosses the intended track, but has changed heading so drastically that it crosses at a very steep angle to the desired heading. Before it can recover, the boat is off course quite a distance to the right. The computer then reports an off-course error to starboard, the autopilot responds by turning hard to port, and the cycle

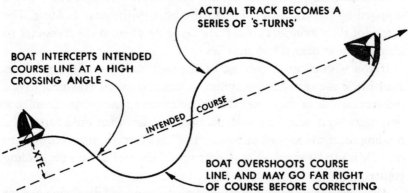

ACTUAL TRACK BECOMES A
SERIES OF 'S-TURNS'

BOAT INTERCEPTS INTENDED
COURSE LINE AT A HIGH
CROSSING ANGLE

INTENDED COURSE

XTE

BOAT OVERSHOOTS COURSE
LINE, AND MAY GO FAR RIGHT
OF COURSE BEFORE CORRECTING

Figure 49 | Engaging the autopilot when the boat is some distance off course may cause the boat to make large "S" turns around the intended course line.

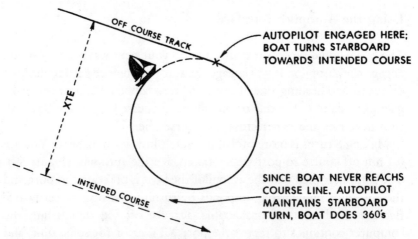

OFF COURSE TRACK

XTE

AUTOPILOT ENGAGED HERE;
BOAT TURNS STARBOARD
TOWARDS INTENDED COURSE

INTENDED COURSE

SINCE BOAT NEVER REACHS
COURSE LINE, AUTOPILOT
MAINTAINS STARBOARD
TURN, BOAT DOES 360's

Figure 50 | If the boat is grossly off course, or if the autopilot causes a rapid change in heading when attempting to correct to course, the boat may change heading by 180° before crossing the desired course line, and will continue to track in circles.

repeats itself. The magnitude of this gyration depends on how the autopilot and vessel respond to steering commands.

The second possibility, in which the boat tracks in circles, occurs when the boat is so far off course, or the autopilot responds by turning so fast, that the boat actually turns a full 180 degrees without crossing the intended course line; the computer then continues to place the vessel off course to port, and the autopilot maintains a starboard turn attempting to reach the rhumb line (Figure 50).

Some autopilots use a more sophisticated technique to correct for off-course errors: rather than blindly changing the heading until the boat is back on course, they compare the present heading with the bearing to the destination and adjust so that the boat gradually returns to course, intersecting the course line at a relatively shallow angle (generally no greater than 20 degrees). As a result, the boat has little chance of drastically overshooting the rhumb line or turning in circles. By using comparative heading and bearing data, these autopilots are also able to keep the boat on a straight track even if signal reception is impaired.

Exercise caution when underway using an autopilot! Regardless of its level of sophistication, an autopilot is only a dumb, mechanical device that can't think for itself—it does only what you or the computer tells it to do. It will attempt to take you from you present position to any destination you name by the most direct route possible, even if that means passing over rocks, reefs, shoals, or other hazards en route. Aids to navigation should *not* replace the human factor, such as crew watching for other vessels, lobster buoys, etc.

REMOTE DISPLAY

On larger vessels, Loran receivers are usually installed inside the boat, in a location protected from salt spray, heat, and other environmental hazards. But mounting the receiver at the chart table, for example, makes it difficult for the helmsman to obtain continuous updates on cross-track error, range, etc. To aid the helmsman, many Loran manufacturers offer *remote displays*, which, when mounted in the cockpit, allow the person at the helm to have more ready access to steering information.

Remote readouts usually display only the steering data of immediate importance to the helmsman. Other navigation data is generally of greater interest to the navigator than to the person steering the boat.

13 | Waypoints and Waypoint Memory

A *Waypoint* (WPT) is a destination—a single, unique geographic point on the earth's surface. It may be a sea buoy marking a home port channel, a productive fishing hole, a spot on a reef where the coral is particularly attractive, the location of a lobster trap, or merely a point where a change in course is to be made. To be used in Loran-C navigation, the coordinates of a waypoint must be entered as a destination into the navigation computer. Waypoints may be entered in two forms: as Loran-C time differences (TDs) or as latitude/longitude.

Anytime you travel from one place to another, you follow a *route*. A simple route may be nothing more complicated than a straight line to a single destination. This is also the simplest form of waypoint navigation: coordinates for one waypoint are entered as a destination into the computer, and the navigational output of the computer (bearing and range, cross-track error, ETE, ETA, etc.) guides you there (Figure 51).

Upon arrival, if this is not your final destination, you enter coordinates for the next waypoint and start on the next leg of your voyage. Using waypoints in this manner, you are not storing a waypoint in the computer's memory for later use, you are merely using the waypoint in real time and then forgetting it. In this instance, it's not necessary to assign a number to each entered waypoint.

More frequently, however, a voyage will require a more complicated route, navigating to a number of successive waypoints en route to a final destination, with changes in course required from one waypoint to

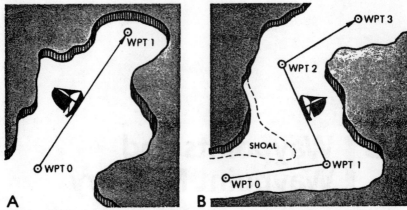

Figure 51 | A route may be very simple, as when you sail directly to a single destination (A), or more complicated, as when navigating to intermediate waypoints on your way to a destination.

another. To use Loran-C in this manner, waypoints must be permanently stored in the computer and a number assigned to each.

WAYPOINT MEMORY

All Loran receivers have a storage feature called *waypoint memory*, in which the coordinates of a number of waypoints are permanently stored. The navigation computer can be told to use stored waypoints in negotiating planned routes, or you can recall a single waypoint from memory for use as a single destination.

Coordinates are stored in a specific place in memory defined by an *address*. For the computer to be able to recall a particular waypoint from memory, the waypoint and its memory address must be assigned a number. Any number may be used, as long as it is within the total number of addresses in memory. Memory capacity varies with the make and model of receiver: some store as few as 10 separate waypoints, others can store up to 100.

Once you have assigned a number to a specific waypoint, be careful not to enter another waypoint using that same number; doing so erases the coordinates of the old waypoint as the new waypoint is recorded over it.

In addition to the number, some Loran receivers allow you to key in a short description of a particular waypoint. In other words, you can describe WPT 20 as a "great Tarpon hole" or WPT 42 as the "center of the Bayway Bridge" to remind you why you wanted to remember that waypoint in the first place. If your receiver doesn't allow you to store information about the waypoint, you should note the description in your Loran logbook.

When entering the coordinates of a destination, press the WPT key. Then, key in the number you want to assign to this WPT (if a previous waypoint has been assigned this number, the coordinates of the old WPT will appear on the readout; make sure to enter them in your logbook if you think you'll ever want to use them again); the number you assign is limited by the number of addresses in memory. Some receivers require you to tell the computer that you are entering coordinates as TDs; in this case, the key would be labeled TD. Key in the time differences of the first TD that defines the waypoint in microseconds and tenths using the numeric keypad (use the CLEAR key to change your entry if you make a mistake), then execute the command by pressing the ENTER key. The time difference will appear in the top readout display window. Repeat the process to enter the second TD. Pressing the WPT key a second time will shift the readout to the lower display window.

You can enter the same position as lat/long coordinates using a similar procedure. Enter the latitude first.

WAYPOINT ZERO

A vessel's present position is constantly fed to the navigation computer by the receiver section of the Loran unit. Most models store present position coordinates in memory as *waypoint zero*. No other coordinates can be stored in this address.

RECALLING WAYPOINTS FROM MEMORY

You can recall or display the coordinates of any waypoint at any time without erasing or altering them or affecting any navigation function, even if the computer is currently using another waypoint for navigation.

By using the *recall* function, you can verify the coordinates of a waypoint for accuracy or correctness or check which waypoint is stored in a particular address while planning your route. Simply press the RECALL key, enter the waypoint number, and execute the command. The TDs, or lat/long, of the waypoint will be displayed.

TEMPORARY MEMORY

Many Loran receivers enable you to store your present position as a waypoint, a feature called the *"save"* or *"hold"* function. The coordinates are held in a group of *temporary* memory addresses and can later be stored in permanent memory. This feature is particularly useful for man-overboard situations and for the immediate storage of a location you are passing that you wish to return to later. On most receivers with this function, simply pushing the SAVE or HOLD button causes the coordinates displayed on the readout at that time to be stored in a temporary memory address; the coordinates can be later recalled for review and stored in permanent memory as a waypoint if desired.

Temporary memory usually has very limited storage capacity. Many receivers, for example, use only the WPT 99 permanent storage address as the *save* address, thus limiting temporary storage to one waypoint. In this case, the coordinates held in WPT 99 should be recalled and stored in a different memory address before the SAVE button is pushed again; otherwise, the old coordinates will be erased. If your receivers uses a permanent waypoint address for temporary storage, it's a good idea to reserve it for that use and avoid storing permanent waypoint data there.

Some receivers provide several addresses dedicated strictly to temporary storage; most such units offer about ten, although some provide more. When a new present position is saved on many of these units, it is stored in the next available address until all temporary addresses are full. Then, when another position is added, it is stored in the lowest numerical address, and the old contents of that address are erased. Some receivers, though, allow you to specify an address in which to store a new waypoint.

Present position coordinates are always entered into temporary memory as LOPs, read as time differences directly from the receiver readout. They can be stored using the save/hold function at any time without affecting navigation functions in progress.

To avoid losing data inadvertently, you should periodically recall waypoints from temporary memory and store them in permanent memory. Decide which permanent memory address you want to use, note the contents of that address in your Loran logbook, and, finally, move the contents of the temporary address to that permanent address. Don't forget to write down old coordinates before you enter (overwrite) new ones—it's frustrating to lose the location of a great fishing hole just because you neglected to write down a waypoint before erasing it.

In addition to storing the coordinates of a position, many receivers also make note of the time at which the waypoint was saved.

BATTERY

Waypoint memory retains coordinates only as long as there is electrical power supplied to the receiver. Many boaters, especially those with open sportfishing boats or runabouts, don't like to leave their Lorans onboard exposed to the weather and the possibility of theft. These boaters remove their receivers from the boat at the end of a voyage to store below or take home for safekeeping. They would find it frustrating to have to put each waypoint back into memory every time they put the receiver back onboard.

A small lithium battery inside the receiver supplies constant power to memory, so waypoints are not lost if the receiver is disconnected from the boat's 12-volt power supply. This battery ensures that the waypoints you've entered, and much additional data, can be retained for several years without the Loran ever being turned on. In many Loran models, the battery enables memory to hold other information, such as the chain and secondaries that were in use when the set was turned off.

These batteries should last up to seven years before wearing out. They do run down eventually, though, and if it happens to you, all the waypoints you've stored in memory will be lost. It's a good idea to periodically check the storage battery. Consult your operator's manual for information on how to replace the battery in your particular model.

LORAN LOGBOOK

Because a Loran's memory storage is limited, it may be necessary to periodically erase old waypoints to make room for new ones. Perhaps WPT 15 had been one of your best fishing spots, but it has petered out and you catch very little there anymore. A new spot you found this afternoon promises to be great, and you want to enter it as a new waypoint. You can easily clear the old coordinates from WPT 15 and enter the TDs or lat/long of the new spot.

Before erasing the old coordinates, however, you may wish to note them in a Loran logbook in case you decide to return to the old fishing spot to see if the fish have started biting again. If you lose the coordinates you may never locate it again! A logbook is the best way to maintain a record of a large number of waypoints and is invaluable for keeping track of all the old waypoints that have been replaced with more current ones.

When entering waypoints in a logbook, write a brief description of what that spot is and why you want to remember it. Giving it a name such as the "tugboat wreck" or "angelfish reef" will jog your memory. You might find it helpful to include information on water depth, the nature of the bottom, the number and kind of fish, weather and sea conditions, and the range and bearing of the waypoint from some known landmark ashore. It's also a good idea to switch to another secondary pair and record a second set of TDs, just in case your primary stations are inoperative the day you want to return.

14 | Basic Waypoint Navigation

Waypoint navigation is perhaps the most frequently used feature of Loran-C. All you do to take advantage of this wonderful feature is enter the coordinates of a destination into the computer. Waypoints may be entered as a single destination, in which case the coordinates are entered directly into the computer without the necessity of assigning the waypoint a number, or as multiple destinations to be stored in memory for future recall.

This chapter covers the simplest form of waypoint navigation, getting from your present position to a single destination waypoint. Chapter 15 discusses route planning and the more complicated process of navigating to sequential waypoints.

Let's assume that your present position is at W—12390.0, Y—45605.0 in chain 7980, position A, and that you wish to go directly from A to WPT 7 (Figure 52). The most important information you need is the course to steer (bearing) and distance to the destination (range). Other important information includes your actual course and speed (CMG/SMG), any deviations you make from your intended course (XTE), and the time left to travel (ETE).

It's interesting to note that the navigation computer calculates bearings and ranges as *great circle* courses and distances on the earth's surface, which are slightly different from straight line or rhumb line courses and distances. If, for example, your voyage includes a leg that's over 200 miles long, you'll find that the bearing to your destination changes slightly but continuously as you proceed along the course; this is because the great circle you are following is actually a curved line on the standard nautical chart. The change in bearing is noticeable only for long east-west legs; north-south headings are predominantly along great circles anyway.

To determine bearing and range, press the FROM/TO key or your model's equivalent. Enter your present position as WPT 0. Then enter the TDs for your destination, or, if the waypoint is already stored in memory, enter the number under which it is stored. If you were entering information based on the example in Figure 52, the computer would respond by displaying the bearing and range to WPT 7. Bearing is 064 degrees and range is 29 nm.

Remember, bearings are expressed as *true* unless you have entered the local variation into the computer, and to calculate a compass course for the helmsman, you must also correct for deviation. In this example, you've entered a local variation of 2 degrees east, so the 064 displayed on the readout is the *magnetic* bearing to WPT 7. Checking the deviation table for your boat, you find the deviation on this heading to be 4 degrees east; subtracting 4 from 064 gives you a compass course of 060.

As you proceed, the bearing should remain the same and the range should decrease, indicating that you are still on the rhumb line from your original WPT 0 (A) and getting closer to WPT 7. (In this example, with the initial range only 29 nm, the rhumb line course and the great circle

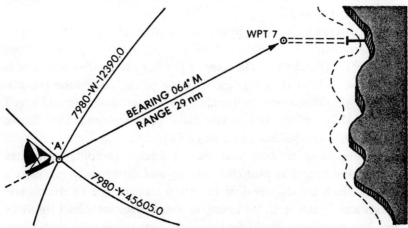

Figure 52 | Navigating to a single destination waypoint.

course are for practical purposes the same.) If the bearing changes, it's an indication that you have strayed from the rhumb line; in other words, your course made good (CMG) is not the same as your intended track.

At point B you check range and bearing by pressing the FROM/TO key and find that the bearing has changed to 057 magnetic (059 true) and the range has decreased to 24 nautical miles. Your boat has strayed from the 064 rhumb line that the computer is using as a reference but has gotten 5 nm closer to WPT 7. Something has set your boat south of the rhumb line. If you had used your Loran to determine your course made good (CMG), your boat's actual track over the bottom, you would have known that what your boat was actually doing was not what you thought it was doing. If queried, the CMG function will tell you that your actual track has been 069 magnetic, rather than the 064 you thought you were making. Simply press the CMG key, then press ENTER. The SMG function will indicate that you have been making 6.9 knots over the bottom, rather than the 8.0 knots shown on your knotmeter. You know, then, that currents, leeway, or other influences have set you south of your intended course line, but how *far* south? The course deviation

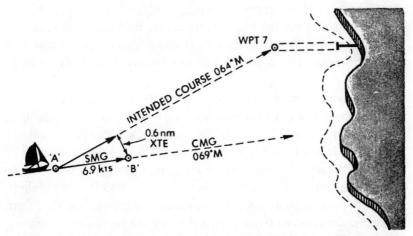

Figure 53 | Currents, steering errors, or leeway have set the boat south of the rhumb line, as indicated by a change in the bearing to WPT 7; the course deviation indicator shows the boat to be 0.6 nm south of her intended track.

indicator (CDI) can tell you. The CDI displays cross track error (XTE), which tells you if you are off course, and if so, by how much. Having noticed that the bearing to WPT 7 has changed, you switch to the XTE mode on the computer (press XTE, then ENTER), and in this case it will tell you that you are 0.6 nm right of course, and must steer left to return.

How do you interpret the XTE display? Cross track error is computed perpendicular to the original rhumb line. On most models, the amount and direction of error are displayed rather directly; the readout tells you that you are 0.6 nm off the rhumb line, and the fact that the 0.6 is off-center to the *right* indicates that you must steer *left* to get back on course. The display appears as follows:

$$\boxed{ .6 }$$

If you are on course, two centered zeros are displayed. If numbers appear on the left side of the readout, you are off course to port.

Most receivers display off-course errors in increments of 0.1 nm and provide port or starboard steering information. Some receivers display XTE to 0.01 nm, or about 60 feet. Although it seems redundant and hardly necessary, some receivers feature, in addition to the XTE display, a graphic steering display, which is intended to help you visualize how to return to course. Figure 54 shows a few examples of the various ways steering indicators are displayed. You may find the XTE display easier to use.

The major factors causing off-course errors are current set and drift, an improperly calibrated compass, steering errors, and leeway (crabbing sideways downwind). Whatever the causes, you know in our current example that you are off course by 0.6 nm and must decide whether to return to the rhumb line before resuming your passage to WPT 7 or to proceed directly from where you are. You may find it worthwhile to return to your original course if it is necessary to approach WPT 7 from a specific direction to avoid obstructions or the possibility of running aground (Figure 55). On the other hand, if your destination is a sea buoy into your home channel, and it is surrounded by deep water, there is no reason to approach the buoy from any particular direction. In this case, you can proceed directly from point B (Figure 56).

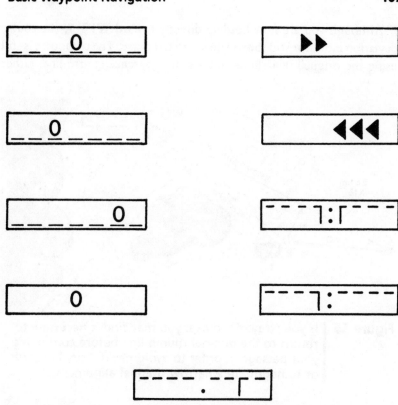

Figure 54 | Examples of steering indicator displays.

If you decide to proceed directly, check the readout to determine the present bearing and range to your destination. In the above illustration, the readout shows the following:

$$\boxed{057 \quad 24}$$

WPT 7 bears 057 magnetic at a range of 24 nm from point B. To go directly from B to WPT 7, alter course to a compass heading of 053 degrees (057 magnetic minus 4 east deviation). As long as you remain on the new 053 rhumb line (compensating, of course, for currents, steering errors, and leeway), the bearing will remain constant and the range will decrease.

Although you are now heading directly toward WPT 7, the course deviation indicator still shows you south of course. The computer is still using the original 064 rhumb line as the reference course line, rather

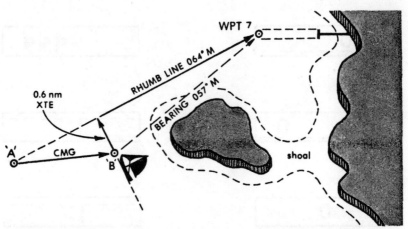

Figure 55 | If you stray off course, you may find it necessary to return to the original rhumb line before continuing your passage in order to avoid navigational hazards or to negotiate a narrow channel alignment.

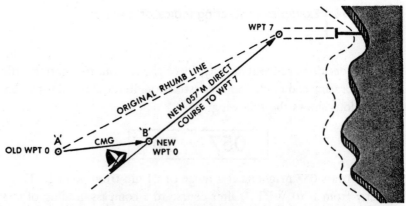

Figure 56 | If there are no navigational hazards, you may decide to sail directly to your destination. To get updated steering and off course information from the computer, you should clear the old rhumb line and enter the new course line.

than your new 053 course line. In order to make effective use of the XTE display, anytime you choose to change headings, you must let the navigation computer know by zeroing out the cross track error and defining a new WPT 0; this tells the computer to calculate a new rhumb line from your new present position and display steering errors in reference to this new course line. The new rhumb line is entered the same way as the original rhumb line was. Press the FROM/TO key, define your new WPT 0, define the destination waypoint (WPT 7), and execute the command by pressing ENTER. Bearing and range data are shown. If you then press XTE and then ENTER, the displayed XTE will become zero, showing that you are on your newly defined course.

All this manipulation of present position and destination waypoints may seem confusing at first, but after you have used the computer to calculate bearing and range, or CMG/SMG, or used the course deviation indicator and graphic steering display a few times, the procedures become second nature.

Underway for WPT 7 once again, you keep a watchful eye on the course deviation indicator and use it to stay very near the rhumb line. In so doing, you can automatically correct for the effects of current, steering errors, etc.

You are making good speed, and not long after leaving point B you decide to find out how long it will be before you arrive at your destination. By pushing the appropriate buttons, you can have the computer calculate both your estimated time en route (ETE) and your estimated time of arrival (ETA).

As you near WPT 7, the arrival alarm sounds, indicating that you are within 0.5 nm of your destination. You have completed a successful passage from your original point of departure to a destination waypoint, with only one minor digression from course. This is the simplest form of waypoint navigation, but during such a passage you would use many of the navigational features of your computer: range and bearing, cross track error, steering indicator, course/speed made good, estimated time en route and of arrival, and the arrival alarm. After making several passages, you'll find using the computer to provide this range of navigation information to be quite easy.

15 | Routes and Route Planning

The previous chapter covered basic waypoint navigation and how to use the navigation computer to remain on course between one waypoint and another. An amazing little device, the nav—and it has even more tricks up its sleeve. Not only can it guide you to a single waypoint, it also allows you to define a *route*, a series of waypoints that leads to a final destination, and it can automatically guide you along the route from one waypoint to the next, until you arrive at your destination.

You can define a number of routes and store them in the computer's memory. They then can be recalled, eliminating the trouble of redefining a particular route each time you need to use it. Stored routes are retained in memory even when the receiver is turned off.

The computer's ability to remember routes makes Loran-C navigation quite easy. Route planning can be done well in advance of embarking on the cruise, and once underway, the computer automatically sequences from one waypoint to the next, which relieves the navigator of having to enter the coordinates of the next waypoint each time the boat arrives at the current waypoint.

Routes can serve a variety of purposes:

- They allow you to steer your boat precisely from one point to another (point-to-point navigation).

- They make repeating a route much easier, such as negotiating your entrance channel or returning to the same diving spot several days in a row.

- They make it easy to follow the same route on your trip home that was used on the way out.

And routes are flexible. At any point, you may deviate from the originally planned route and return to it later, if you wish.

ROUTE LOG

It's a good idea to note the various waypoints in a specific route in detail in a *route log*, similar to a waypoint logbook. Include the GRI of the chain being used, a brief description of the overall route, the reason for saving it, and the coordinates of each waypoint. Briefly describe the particulars of each turning point. Maintaining a route log will make route navigation much easier and will prevent a lot of confusion.

ROUTE STORAGE

The number of routes that can be stored in the nav computer varies with the make and model of receiver. Some store as few as 10, some as many as 99. The combined number of waypoints in all stored routes, however, cannot exceed the capacity of waypoint memory. For example, if your receiver has a maximum waypoint memory capacity of 100 waypoints, you could define two routes containing 50 waypoints each or 20 routes of 5 waypoints each.

There are three ways to define a route:

- *Store:* the coordinates of each waypoint are entered into the computer in advance. This form of route storage involves entering the coordinates of a series of waypoints by referring to a chart while planning the trip.

- *Save:* the waypoints are entered one at a time as you navigate a route. You would be using this kind of route storage if, while heading for port, you entered the TDs of each point where you make a course change along the harbor entrance channel, with an eye toward following the same route back out to sea.

- *Define:* miscellaneous waypoints stored in waypoint memory are organized into a route.

You can follow a stored route in both directions, either going or coming—for example, following a route from your home port to your favorite fishing area and reversing it to go back home.

A route number is assigned to each series of waypoints for the computer to reference in recalling it for use.

Storing

If a stored route is entirely within the coverage area of a single Loran-C chain, the waypoints defining the route may be entered either as TDs or as lat/long coordinates. If, on the other hand, the route spans the coverage areas of two or more chains, the waypoints must be entered as lat/long coordinates. Time differences are unique to the individual transmitters in a particular chain, and the computer cannot use TDs for one chain while the receiver is tracking signals from another.

The operator's manual for each receiver gives specific instructions for storing routes. The general procedure is to put the computer into the "store route" mode, assign a number to the route, and enter the coordinates of each waypoint in sequential order. If you make a mistake entering the coordinates of a waypoint, press the CLEAR key and enter that waypoint again. When the waypoint sequence is completed, take the computer out of the "store route" mode with the appropriate keystrokes.

Saving

When the *save* method of storing a route is used, coordinates are not taken off a chart or obtained from a friend. Waypoints on a saved route are found directly by passing over them. They are defined by the actual TDs or lat/long of a position at the time your boat is at that position.

The coordinates are entered directly into memory from the readout when the SAVE ROUTE key is pressed; this is much the same as defining present position as a waypoint, as discussed in Chapter 13. "Saving" waypoints is an ideal way of defining a route, since in doing so you must actually navigate the route and obtain the true coordinates of each waypoint. It is much more accurate than interpolating TDs or lat/long from a chart and "storing" them.

Saving a route generally consists of putting the computer into the "save route" mode, assigning a number to the route, and pressing the SAVE key whenever the boat reaches a waypoint. When the last waypoint in the route has been entered, exit the "save route" mode.

Generally, if the receiver is turned off while in the "save route" mode, it will still be in that mode when it is turned on again, and pressing the SAVE key will store the TDs or lat/long displayed at the time as a continuing part of the same route.

Defining

A third way of creating a route is to use waypoints that have already been stored in memory. For example, assume that you have waypoints 4, 11, 15, and 22 stored in waypoint memory as separate destinations (not as a route). You now wish, however, to define a route using these four waypoints. The route function of the computer is able to recall these individual points from its memory and organize them into a specified order.

Suppose that you want to travel from WPT 15 to WPT 4, then to WPT 22, and finally to WPT 11. The procedure for defining a route is very similar to the one used to store a route. Instead of entering coordinates, however, you simply enter the number for each waypoint in the proper sequence. Waypoints stored as a defined route can still be used as separate destinations.

Adding Waypoints to a Route

To add waypoints within or at the end of an existing route, simply press the SAVE ROUTE or STORE ROUTE key and enter the number of the route. The computer will warn you that the route already exists, but it will nevertheless allow waypoints to be added to the route.

If you wish to add waypoint coordinates without actually navigating to the position, use the "store route" feature, and enter each waypoint as described above. If you want to add new waypoints as you reach them, use the "save route" function and press the SAVE key at the desired waypoints.

New waypoints are usually appended at the end of an existing route. If you want to start a whole new route, press CLEAR and enter a route number that has not already been assigned, or "erase" an existing route.

NAVIGATING A ROUTE

Stored routes can be recalled and used at any time by specifying the route number. The receiver will provide steering and navigational information from the first waypoint through the entire series of waypoints along the route.

Most receivers will ask if you wish to follow the route forward or in reverse. If you go forward, the computer begins by displaying the first waypoint entered and then takes you sequentially through the entire series of intermediate waypoints in the order in which they were entered. If you elect to follow the route in reverse, the computer begins with the last waypoint entered and follows the same series in reverse order. The

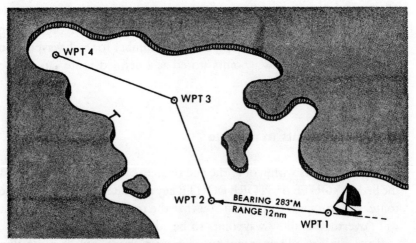

Figure 57 | After recalling a particular route on the computer and indicating direction of travel, simply follow the steering directions presented.

commands to indicate direction are explained in the operator's manual.

Once you have told the computer to recall a certain route and have indicated the direction you want to take that route, you simply follow the steering directions presented by the computer. Keep an eye on the cross-track error, occasionally check the bearing and range to the next waypoint, and ask the computer for CMG, SMG, VMG, ETE, ETA, and the other navigational functions as you normally would (Figure 57). As soon as you are within 0.1 nm (the radius of the arrival alarm) of WPT 2, the alarm will sound. When you actually arrive at WPT 2, one of two things happens:

- You instruct the computer to shift navigation priority to the next waypoint in the route sequence, WPT 3, by pressing the ROUTE key and then pressing ENTER, for example. The computer then displays steering information to WPT 3.

- If you are making use of a feature called "automatic waypoint sequencing," the computer will, upon arriving at WPT 2, automatically shift navigation priority to WPT 3. Thereafter, steering data to the *next* waypoint along the route are displayed.

PASSING A WAYPOINT

If you are not using an autopilot to keep on track, it's possible that you could get somewhat off course. If so, you might not actually get to the waypoint, instead passing it some distance off. A waypoint is considered "passed" when the boat crosses an imaginary line drawn through the waypoint perpendicular to the course line you have been on (Figure 58).

If you pass a waypoint, many receivers will warn you by producing an audible beep or displaying a message on the readout. If you are using the automatic waypoint sequencing mode, the computer will, upon crossing the imaginary line, automatically shift navigation priority to the next waypoint. If you are not using the automatic sequencing, the steering and range/bearing displays will still reference the passed point and you must manually shift priority to the next waypoint.

NAVIGATING FROM AN OFF-COURSE POSITION

There may be times when you deviate from the intended rhumb line between one waypoint and another, either to avoid an obstacle on your course line or because you wandered off course. Whatever the reason, there are two ways to reach your next waypoint. You can use the cross-track error function and steering display to guide you back to the rhumb line, or, if there is not reason to return to the original course line, you may decide to proceed directly to the next waypoint from your off-course position. If you decide to proceed directly and you wish to use steering and cross-track error information based on your present position, you must reset the computer so it uses your new course line as a reference instead of the old rhumb line. This can be done without changing any of the stored waypoints. Most receivers have a feature that provides for this situation, and when used it resets the computer's XTE and steering displays to the new course (Figure 59). The terminology and keystrokes required to use this feature vary with the receiver: it may be called RESTART, or START HERE, or a similar term. When you

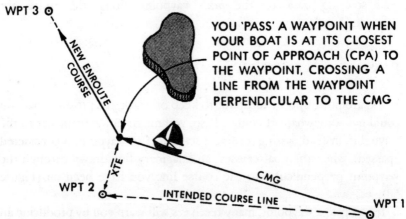

Figure 58 | You are considered to have "passed" a waypont when your boat crosses an imaginary line extending from the waypoint perpendicular to the course line just traveled. In the automatic waypoint sequencing mode, the computer automatically shifts navigational priority to the next waypoint on the route.

arrive at the next waypoint, the computer will switch navigational priority as though you had never been off course at all.

DIVERTING FROM A ROUTE

Often an opportunity arises to do something interesting that doesn't happen to lie directly on your scheduled course line. You decide to check out a little cove that looks like a cozy anchorage, for example, or you see the mast of an old wreck protruding from the water and want to stop for a quick investigative dive. With Loran-assisted navigation, you can divert from your planned route, travel to another point, and then return to the original route. This is done by overriding the waypoint to which you were originally steering and telling the computer to calculate a course to the new point (Figure 60).

To divert from a planned route, use a function named something like DIVERT or STEER TO NEW POINT. If you know the coordinates of the new point, key them into the computer and it will calculate bearing and range to the point, XTE, steering information, etc.

When you are ready to return to your original course line, cancel the "divert" mode with the appropriate command (CANCEL DIVERT, CANCEL NEW POINT, etc.). The steering and XTE information displayed will refer to your original course and assist you in returning to it.

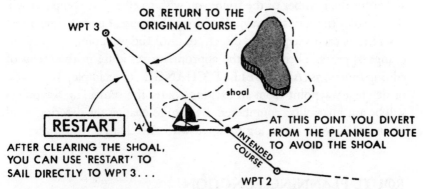

Figure 59 | Proceeding to the next waypoint from an off-course position; the RESTART feature is used to reset the XTE and steering displays to the new course line.

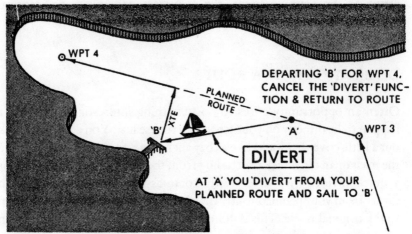

Figure 60 | Use the DIVERT function to divert from your original course, then use the nav functions of the computer to steer to the new point; cancel the DIVERT function and use XTE and steering displays to return to your original course line.

EDITING A ROUTE

There may be occasions when you'll wish to modify, or *edit*, an existing route. This may involve changing the sequence of points, inserting new waypoints, or deleting old ones. Key the computer into the "edit" mode, and enter the number of the route you wish to edit. The computer will then display the series of waypoints along the route, one at a time. Press ENTER as each waypoint is displayed, until the waypoint you wish to change appears. Then select the appropriate response in the menu of editing functions (ADD, DELETE, CHANGE, for example). If you add or delete a waypoint from an existing route, the remaining waypoints will be automatically renumbered. Be sure to change the description of the route in your route log to agree with any changes you make.

ROUTE PLANNING FUNCTION

The "route planning" function of the navigation computer provides a handy way to get an overall view of an existing route. This function displays the bearing and range from each waypoint to the next and the total distance along the route.

When using the route planning mode, you must first ensure that the receiver is set to the same GRI that was in use when the waypoints were saved. If the displayed bearings are magnetic, the variation used to calculate the bearings is that of the area covered by the route, not of the area in which you are presently operating.

By using the appropriate keystrokes, you can get the computer to display bearing and range information for each waypoint, in sequence. After the last waypoint, the computer displays the cumulative distance from the first waypoint, through all the intermediate waypoints, to the last.

CANCELLING A ROUTE

Cancelling a route that is being used for navigation merely terminates the display of the route function on the readout; it does not erase the route from memory. The cancelled route may be recalled at any time.

You can cancel only the route that is currently in use. It is not necessary to cancel a route when you have reached your final destination unless the computer is using the route function to direct the operation of an autopilot. A route is automatically canceled if you shift to another route or if the receiver is turned off.

ERASING A ROUTE

Erasing a route, unlike cancelling a route, permanently erases all the waypoints on the route from memory and clears space for a new route. Erasing a route is *permanent*. Make certain that you really want to *erase*, and then don't until you have entered the coordinates of the waypoints in your route log.

Most computers will not allow you to erase a route you are currently following; you must cancel the route first, then erase it. You also cannot erase a route you are in the process of storing.

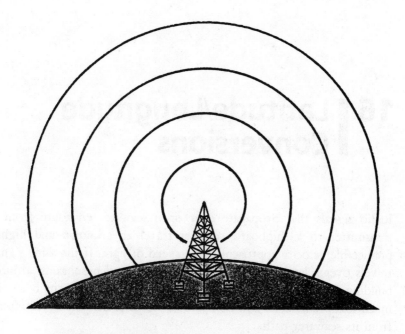

SECTION THREE

Advanced Operations

16 | Latitude/Longitude Conversions

Radio signals that propagate over open seawater en route from a transmitter to a shipboard receiver travel at a known and highly predictable velocity approaching the speed of light. If the same signal travels over a landmass, however—over hills and mountains, around buildings and bridges, over forests—it slows down, its velocity becomes much less predictable, and its route of travel is deflected (refracted) from its seawater path.

Traveling at the seawater velocity of 0.162 nm per microsecond, for example, a Loran pulse covers a distance of 162.0 nautical miles in 1,000 microseconds; a pulse slowed by land path effects may cover only 161.0 nautical miles in the same time. The 1000 ms TD on an older Loran-C chart would have been printed 162.0 nm from the transmitter, based on the distance traveled at the seawater velocity, while its actual location would be 1 nautical mile *closer* to the transmitter. In such a case, if your receiver displays a TD of 1000 ms and you plot your position on the 1000 ms LOP on an older chart, you will appear to be 1 nautical mile farther from the transmitter than you actually are.

When Loran-C was developed, engineers were faced with the problem of where to locate the LOPs on the charts. They knew that all Loran transmitters are located inland along the coast, and signals therefore always travel over both land *and* sea paths to reach receivers within a coverage area, so it was clear that all signals actually travel at a velocity *slower* than the ideal seawater velocity. In those early days, however, there was not enough time, manpower, or money to field

122

check the actual geographic locations of LOPs before they were printed on Loran-C charts, so the engineers used the short-cut assumption that *all* Loran-C signals travel exclusively over open ocean. As a result, most of the LOPs on early charts were more or less in error. If you use an older Loran-C chart, you must apply a correction in order to make your plotted position agree with your actual position.

There are two categories of signal propagation errors that can affect the accuracy of your position: Secondary Phase Factors (SF) and Additional Secondary Phase Factors (ASF).

SECONDARY PHASE FACTORS (SF)

The velocity decrease of a radio signal as it propagates over open ocean is well known; the *predictable* change in Loran-C time differences caused by this known change in velocity, called the Secondary Phase Factor (SF), was taken into account when LOPs were first plotted on charts. Most receivers are also programmed with a highly detailed model of the actual SFs within Loran coverage areas, and automatically compensate for SF when converting TDs to their corresponding latitude/longitude coordinates. These automatic compensations for SF are, however, less reliable when you are operating very close to or at great distances from a transmitter.

ADDITIONAL SECONDARY PHASE FACTORS (ASF)

Additional Secondary Phase Factors (ASF) are the *unpredictable* effects of land paths on time differences. Within a Loran coverage area, changes in signal velocity due to land path effects vary depending on the percentage of land versus seawater along the signal path. The two transmitters of the secondary pair used to plot a fix are located in different parts of the coverage area, so the signals from each travel a different path to arrive at your boat. Land path effects also vary according to the ruggedness of the terrain the signal traverses, the type of ground cover, etc. Therefore, the ASFs and the required corrections will be different for each secondary, and cannot be predicted from theory; they must be determined empirically.

ASF corrections range from −9.9 microseconds to +9.9 microseconds, and are listed in the Defense Mapping Agency publication "Loran-C Correction Tables" (Figures 61 and 62). The book contains separate tables for each chain in the Loran-C system and for each secondary transmitter within a chain. Each table is divided into sections, each section covering three degrees of latitude and one degree of longitude. ASF correction tables may be ordered from:

> Defense Mapping Agency
> Hydrographic/Topographic Center
> Washington, DC 20315

7980-W

LAT	84°0'	55	50	45	40	35	30	25	20	15	10	5	83°0
30° 0'	−0.7	−0.7											
55	−0.7	−0.7	−0.7	−0.6									
50	−0.8	−0.7	−0.8	−0.7	−0.6								
45	−0.7	−0.6	−0.6	−0.6	−0.6	−0.6							
40	−0.6	−0.5	−0.6	−0.6	−0.6	−0.6	−0.4	−0.1					
35	−0.5	−0.5	−0.5	−0.5	−0.5	−0.5	−0.5	−0.5					
30	−0.4	−0.4	−0.4	−0.4	−0.5	−0.5	−0.5	−0.4					
25	−0.3	−0.4	−0.4	−0.4	−0.4	−0.4	−0.5	−0.4	−0.4	−0.3			
20	−0.2	−0.3	−0.3	−0.4	−0.3	−0.3	−0.4	−0.4	−0.5	−0.4	−0.3		
15	−0.3	−0.3	−0.2	−0.4	−0.2	−0.3	−0.3	−0.4	−0.4	−0.3	−0.3	−0.2	
10	−0.3	−0.3	−0.3	−0.4	−0.2	−0.2	−0.2	−0.4	−0.3	−0.3	−0.3	−0.2	
5	−0.2	−0.2	−0.2	−0.2	−0.2	−0.3	−0.3	−0.4	−0.3	−0.2	−0.3	−0.3	−0.2
29° 0'	−0.2	−0.2	−0.2	−0.2	−0.2	−0.2	−0.2	−0.2	−0.2	−0.3	−0.4	−0.5	−0.3
55	−0.1	−0.2	−0.2	−0.2	−0.2	−0.2	−0.2	−0.2	−0.2	−0.2	−0.2	−0.2	−0.3
50	−0.1	−0.2	−0.1	−0.2	−0.1	−0.2	−0.2	−0.2	−0.2	−0.2	−0.2	−0.2	−0.2
45	−0.1	−0.1	−0.1	−0.2	−0.1	−0.2	−0.2	−0.2	−0.2	−0.2	−0.2	−0.2	−0.3
40	−0.1	−0.1	−0.1	−0.1	−0.2	−0.1	−0.1	−0.1	−0.1	−0.2	−0.2	−0.2	−0.2
35	−0.1	−0.2	−0.2	−0.2	−0.2	−0.1	−0.1	−0.1	−0.1	−0.2	−0.2	−0.2	−0.2
30	−0.1	−0.2	−0.1	−0.2	−0.2	−0.2	−0.2	−0.2	−0.2	−0.2	−0.2	−0.2	−0.2
25	−0.2	−0.2	−0.2	−0.2	−0.2	−0.2	−0.2	−0.2	−0.2	−0.2	−0.2	−0.2	−0.2
20	−0.2	−0.2	−0.2	−0.1	−0.2	−0.2	−0.2	−0.2	−0.2	−0.2	−0.2	−0.2	−0.2
15	−0.2	−0.2	−0.2	−0.2	−0.2	−0.2	−0.2	−0.2	−0.2	−0.2	−0.2	−0.2	−0.2
10	−0.2	−0.2	−0.2	−0.2	−0.2	−0.2	−0.2	−0.2	−0.2	−0.2	−0.2	−0.2	−0.2
5	−0.2	−0.2	−0.2	−0.2	−0.2	−0.2	−0.2	−0.2	−0.2	−0.2	−0.2	−0.2	−0.2
28° 0'	−0.2	−0.2	−0.2	−0.2	−0.2	−0.2	−0.2	−0.2	−0.2	−0.2	−0.2	−0.2	−0.1
55	−0.2	−0.2	−0.2	−0.2	−0.2	−0.2	−0.2	−0.2	−0.2	−0.2	−0.2	−0.2	−0.2
50	−0.2	−0.2	−0.2	−0.2	−0.2	−0.2	−0.2	−0.2	−0.2	−0.2	−0.2	−0.2	−0.1
45	−0.2	−0.2	−0.2	−0.2	−0.2	−0.2	−0.2	−0.2	−0.2	−0.2	−0.2	−0.2	−0.2
40	−0.2	−0.2	−0.2	−0.2	−0.2	−0.2	−0.2	−0.2	−0.2	−0.2	−0.1	−0.2	−0.2
35	−0.2	−0.2	−0.2	−0.2	−0.2	−0.2	−0.2	−0.2	−0.2	−0.2	−0.1	−0.2	−0.2
30	−0.1	−0.1	−0.1	−0.2	−0.1	−0.2	−0.2	−0.2	−0.2	−0.2	−0.2	−0.2	−0.2
25	−0.1	−0.1	−0.1	−0.1	−0.1	−0.1	−0.1	−0.2	−0.2	−0.2	−0.2	−0.2	−0.2
20	−0.1	−0.1	−0.1	−0.1	−0.1	−0.1	−0.1	−0.2	−0.2	−0.2	−0.2	−0.2	−0.2
15	−0.1	−0.1	−0.1	−0.1	−0.1	−0.1	−0.1	−0.1	−0.2	−0.2	−0.2	−0.2	−0.2
10	−0.1	−0.1	−0.1	−0.1	−0.1	−0.1	−0.1	−0.1	−0.1	−0.1	−0.2	−0.2	−0.2
5	−0.1	−0.1	−0.1	−0.1	−0.1	−0.1	−0.1	−0.1	−0.1	−0.1	−0.1	−0.2	−0.2
27° 0'	−0.1	−0.1	−0.1	−0.1	−0.1	−0.1	−0.1	−0.1	−0.1	−0.1	−0.1	−0.1	−0.1

Figure 61 | Loran-C ASF Correction Table for 7980-W Secondary for latitudes 27-30° North, longitudes 83-84° West.

Ask for DMA Stock Number LCPUB 2211200-C.

The ASF corrections in these tables, often called TD Offsets, represent the difference in microseconds between the TD that is actually displayed on a Loran receiver (based on the *actual* velocity of a signal as it passes over a combination of seawater and landmasses en route to a boat) and the TD predicted at that location using the idealized seawater velocity.

Plotting the LOP that exactly corresponds to the TD on the receiver on older Loran-C charts, without making corrections for ASF from the

7980-Y

LATITUDE NORTH	84° 0'	55	50	45	40	35	30	25	20	15	10	5	83° 0
30° 0'	-0.1	-0.2											
55	-0.1	-0.2	-0.2	-0.3									
50	-0.0	-0.2	-0.3	-0.3	-0.4								
45	-0.0	-0.0	-0.1	-0.2	-0.3	-0.4							
40	-0.0	-0.0	-0.1	-0.1	-0.2	-0.2	-0.3	-0.2					
35	-0.0	-0.0	-0.0	-0.1	-0.1	-0.2	-0.5						
30	-0.0	-0.0	-0.0	-0.0	-0.1	-0.1	-0.2	-0.3					
25	-0.0	-0.0	-0.0	-0.0	-0.1	-0.1	-0.1	-0.1	-0.2	-0.1			
20	-0.0	-0.0	-0.0	-0.0	-0.0	-0.1	-0.1	-0.1	-0.2	-0.1	-0.1		
15	-0.0	-0.0	-0.0	-0.0	-0.0	-0.0	-0.1	-0.1	-0.2	-0.1	-0.1	-0.2	
10	-0.0	-0.0	-0.0	-0.0	-0.0	-0.0	-0.1	-0.1	-0.1	-0.1	-0.1	-0.2	
5	-0.0	-0.0	-0.0	-0.0	-0.0	-0.0	-0.1	-0.1	-0.1	-0.1	-0.1	-0.2	-0.2
29° 0'	-0.0	-0.0	-0.0	-0.0	-0.0	-0.0	-0.1	-0.1	-0.1	-0.1	-0.1	-0.2	-0.2
55	-0.0	-0.0	-0.0	-0.0	-0.0	-0.0	-0.1	-0.1	-0.1	-0.1	-0.1	-0.1	-0.1
50	-0.0	-0.1	-0.1	-0.1	-0.1	-0.1	-0.1	-0.1	-0.1	-0.1	-0.1	-0.1	-0.1
45	-0.1	-0.1	-0.1	-0.1	-0.1	-0.1	-0.1	-0.1	-0.1	-0.1	-0.1	-0.1	-0.1
40	-0.1	-0.1	-0.1	-0.1	-0.1	-0.1	-0.1	-0.1	-0.1	-0.1	-0.1	-0.1	-0.1
35	-0.1	-0.1	-0.1	-0.1	-0.1	-0.1	-0.1	-0.1	-0.1	-0.1	-0.1	-0.1	-0.1
30	-0.0	-0.0	-0.1	-0.1	-0.1	-0.1	-0.1	-0.1	-0.1	-0.1	-0.1	-0.1	-0.1
25	-0.0	-0.1	-0.1	-0.1	-0.1	-0.1	-0.1	-0.1	-0.1	-0.1	-0.1	-0.2	-0.2
20	-0.0	-0.1	-0.1	-0.0	-0.1	-0.1	-0.1	-0.1	-0.1	-0.1	-0.1	-0.2	-0.2
15	-0.0	-0.1	-0.1	-0.1	-0.1	-0.0	-0.1	-0.0	-0.1	-0.1	-0.1	-0.2	-0.2
10	-0.0	-0.0	-0.1	-0.1	-0.1	-0.0	-0.1	-0.0	-0.1	-0.1	-0.1	-0.1	-0.1
5	-0.0	-0.0	-0.0	-0.1	-0.1	-0.0	-0.1	-0.1	-0.1	-0.1	-0.1	-0.1	-0.1
28° 0'	-0.0	-0.0	-0.0	-0.0	-0.1	-0.1	-0.1	-0.1	-0.1	-0.1	-0.1	-0.1	-0.0
55	-0.0	-0.0	-0.0	-0.0	-0.0	-0.0	-0.1	-0.1	-0.1	-0.1	-0.1	-0.1	-0.2
50	-0.0	-0.0	-0.0	-0.1	-0.0	-0.1	-0.1	-0.1	-0.0	-0.1	-0.1	-0.1	-0.1
45	-0.0	-0.0	-0.0	-0.0	-0.0	-0.1	-0.1	-0.1	-0.0	-0.1	-0.1	-0.0	-0.0
40	-0.0	-0.1	-0.1	-0.1	-0.1	-0.1	-0.1	-0.0	-0.0	-0.0	-0.0	-0.0	-0.1
35	-0.0	-0.0	-0.0	-0.1	-0.1	-0.1	-0.1	-0.0	-0.1	-0.1	-0.1	-0.1	-0.1
30	-0.0	-0.0	-0.0	-0.0	-0.0	-0.0	-0.0	-0.0	-0.1	-0.0	-0.0	-0.1	-0.1
25	0.0	0.0	0.0	0.0	-0.0	-0.0	-0.0	-0.0	-0.0	-0.0	-0.0	-0.0	-0.0
20	0.0	0.0	0.0	0.0	0.0	-0.0	-0.0	-0.0	-0.0	-0.0	-0.0	-0.0	-0.0
15	0.0	0.0	0.0	0.0	0.0	-0.0	-0.0	-0.0	-0.0	-0.0	-0.0	-0.0	-0.0
10	0.0	0.0	0.0	0.0	0.0	0.0	0.0	0.0	-0.0	-0.0	-0.0	-0.0	-0.0
5	0.1	0.0	0.0	0.0	0.0	0.0	0.0	0.0	0.0	0.0	0.0	0.0	0.0
27° 0'	0.1	0.1	0.1	0.0	0.0	0.0	0.0	0.0	0.0	0.0	0.0	0.0	0.0

Figure 62 | Loran-C ASF Correction Table for the 7980-Y Secondary for latitudes 27-30° North, longitudes 83-84° West.

tables, can lead to position errors of up to 2 nautical miles. To avoid this, the navigator should apply the appropriate ASFs to the displayed TDs, in effect "uncorrecting" the TDs to make them conform to the uncorrected LOPs printed on the chart.

However, the problem of position errors caused by improperly charted LOPs has been extensively corrected on current charts, as the following section details.

NOS CHART CALIBRATIONS

The National Ocean Service, a division of the National Oceanic and Atmospheric Administration (NOAA), is responsible for the preparation of Loran-C overprinted charts. Since 1971, when the first "experimental" Loran-C charts were printed, NOS has undertaken a program to calibrate or upgrade them. The goal of the program is to meet the ¼ nautical mile accuracy standard established by the U.S. Coast Guard when Loran-C was adopted as the navigation system for the U.S. coastal zone.

The calibration program has proceeded in various stages, with the charts of some areas receiving priority; for this reason, some Loran charts are more accurate than others. On each chart there is a general information note indicating the degree to which the LOPs on that chart have been calibrated. One version of the note is as follows:

> "Loran-C correction tables published by the Defense Mapping Agency or others should be used with this chart. The lines of position shown are based on assumed all-seawater signal paths. Uncorrected positions may not meet the ¼ nautical mile accuracy criteria established by the U.S. Coast Guard. Mariners are cautioned to use larger scale Loran-C charts where possible."

LOPs on charts bearing this note have not yet been corrected for land path delays. When using such charts, mariners desiring accuracies better than ¼ nautical mile will need to adjust displayed TDs using the appropriate ASFs from the tables. The number of such charts, however, is relatively small.

There are a few charts that probably will never be corrected, these being small-scale charts (1:1,500,000 and smaller) covering large geographic areas. Because these charts—a major portion of which center on areas of deep, open ocean with few navigational hazards—are intended primarily for offshore voyaging, ASF corrections are not considered critical for safe navigation.

On larger scale charts (those covering small geographic areas in greater detail), the need for accuracy increases. On offshore coastal charts between 1:200,000 and 1:1,000,000 in scale, which mariners may use to orient themselves to major landmarks when making a landfall, the method of correction is rather crude: all the printed LOPs in a given chain are shifted the same amount based on the average ASF corrections for that chain over the entire area covered. The corrections are computer generated and are not field verified, as indicated by the general information note on these charts:

> "Loran-C correction tables published by the Defense Mapping Agency or others should not be used with this chart. The lines of position shown have been based on theoretically determined overland signal propagation delays. They have not been verified by comparison with survey data. Every effort has been made to meet the ¼ nautical mile accuracy criteria established by the U.S. Coast Guard. Mariners are cautioned not to rely solely on the lattices in inshore waters."

Because the LOPs on these charts have already been corrected for ASFs, additional corrections from the tables should not be applied. Navigators should be aware, however, that the charted corrections are theoretical, and some degree of error may still remain.

In order to meet the Coast Guard accuracy criteria on even larger scale charts (1:80,000 to 1:200,000), the NOS must verify the magnitude of local ASFs by making accurate field measurements of TDs at numerous points within each charted area. The measurements are sent to the Defense Mapping Agency Hydrographic/Topographic Center (DMAHTC), where they are entered into a computer that uses them to predict ASF corrections at all locations within that area. The DMAHTC uses these computer-generated corrections to update the tables of TD offsets, and then sends them back to the NOS in the form of data tapes containing corrected TD readings for each charted Loran chain at every five minutes of latitude and longitude. The NOS, in turn, plots updated LOPs on new chart editions. Thus, ASF corrections for an entire Loran coverage area are computer-extrapolated from actual TD readings at a relatively few sites. Since the NOS or the Coast Guard is continually field checking additional locations, charted LOPs are constantly refined, coming ever closer to corresponding to their locations in the real world.

The charts on which partially field-verified LOPs are printed bear a general explanation that reads:

> "The Loran-C correction tables published by the Defense Mapping Agency or others should not be used with this chart. The lines of position shown have been adjusted based on survey data. Every effort has been made to meet the ¼ nautical mile accuracy criteria established by the U.S. Coast Guard. Mariners, however, are cautioned not to rely solely on the lattices in inshore waters."

The wording of this explanation has only recently been changed. Older charts contained the following note:

> "The Loran-C lines of position overprinted on this chart have been prepared for use with groundwave signals and are presently compensated only for theoretical propagation delays which have not yet been verified by observed data. Mariners are cautioned not to rely entirely on the lattices in inshore waters."

In any case, additional ASF corrections from the tables should *not* be used with any Loran charts that have already been corrected. Mariners should read the general information note on each chart to determine whether theoretical or surveyed corrections have already been applied.

In the notes, only inshore mariners are cautioned about position errors, because only they require positions of an accuracy to render ASFs critical; offshore sailors are not usually concerned with such minor position errors.

U.S. coastal charts larger than 1:80,000 scale, including harbor and harbor entrance charts, are not currently overprinted with Loran LOPs. This is in part because by definition the Coastal Confluence Zone terminates at a harbor entrance, and in part because of the highly variable nature of ASFs close under the shore, especially within harbors and other restricted waterways. Although the Coast Guard is considering the addition of LOPs to selected large-scale charts in the future, this may have to wait until the NOS develops better methods of verifying ASFs in these waters.

Even on the newest charts, LOPs are located chiefly by computer predictions, and minor disagreements between actual and plotted positions may still occur. Nevertheless, approximately 60 percent of the NOAA charts of the coastal United States in the 1:80,000 to 1:200,000 scale range were corrected based on survey data prior to July 1986. When displayed TDs are plotted on one of these charts, the plotted position will agree closely with a boat's actual position without any additional ASF corrections. The only remaining errors are minor ones caused by small, localized variations in signal speed, which should not amount to more than 0.2 microsecond.

Remaining uncorrected U.S. charts will be revised as processed survey data become available, with priority given to coastal charts. Charts of Lake Erie, Lake Ontario, and Lake Superior are among those still unrevised. In addition, several charts—notably those for Puget Sound and the Straits of Juan de Fuca—have yet to be overprinted with LOPs; these will be revised as survey data permit.

Non–U.S charts are similarly updated as field verifications proceed, although the NOS has no information regarding the specifics of such calibrations. Probably the NOS is ahead of overseas charting agencies in this regard. Many non–U.S. charts larger than 1:250,000 scale are not overprinted with Loran LOPs at all.

CHANGES IN ASF CORRECTIONS

As mentioned, the NOS and the Coast Guard maintain an ongoing program of sampling TDs to calculate actual ASFs. Land path delays, however, are not static; indeed, in many coastal areas they are changing rapidly. Boaters off Florida's west coast have reported noticeable changes in the TDs of many waypoints, particularly when using the "Y" secondary at Jupiter, the pulses from which must cross the peninsula of Florida to reach the Gulf of Mexico. To maintain accuracy, these mariners are constantly updating the TDs of frequently used waypoints. This change in TDs appears to be the result of longer land path delays caused by the increasing number of high-rise buildings along Florida's coastal strand. In any case, the ASF tables for these locations are probably obsolete, albeit to a small extent, before they are printed. This situation may not be an isolated one.

Compounding the problem is the fact that, when NOS field measurements are sent to the DMAHTC for processing, six months may pass before the corrected TDs are returned, and it may take another six months to a year for corrected LOPs to appear on new charts. Therefore, in spite of a considerable overall improvement in chart accuracy, even the most recently printed LOPs may disagree slightly with actual TDs at a specific location. Similarly, the corrections in even the most recent "Loran-C Correction Tables" are subject to minor errors. Boaters should remain vigilant for possible position errors when using Loran in coastal waters.

CONVERTING TIME DIFFERENCES TO LATITUDE/LONGITUDE

Although it may occasionally be necessary to apply ASF corrections to displayed TDs in order to plot a position on an uncorrected chart, the most common use of ASFs is to maintain accuracy when coverting TDs to the corresponding latitude and longitude coordinates.

The nav computer in a Loran receiver is programmed with a highly detailed model of the coverage area, which includes data on the hyperbolic nature of Loran LOPs and the locations of all transmitters in the chain; using this model, the computer is able to calculate the lat/long coordinates of any TD pair. In spite of the sophistication of this model, however, the computer isn't able to determine the land path effect for a specific signal path and thereby use the *actual* speed of propagation *unless* the ASF values from the "Loran-C Correction Tables" have been programmed into the computer by the manufacturer. The more expensive late-model receivers have this capability and will apply the appropriate ASF values automatically when making a conversion. More modestly priced models, however, or those manufactured prior to 1985, may predict the TDs for a given geographic position using the *idealized* speed of signals over open ocean when making a lat/long conversion. Plotting a position based on these lat/long coordinates without first correcting for land path anomalies by applying the appropriate ASF correction will result in position errors. The resultant positions are generally only a short distance from the vessel's actual position, although errors of up to two miles are possible.

The TD Offsets that must be applied when converting TDs to lat/long are found in the same ASF correction tables shown in Figures 61 and 62. When required, manual ASF corrections can be made in one of two ways: corrections may be made to the TDs before the computer makes a lat/long conversion, or lat/long coordinates may be corrected first.

Entering ASF Corrections Directly into the Navigation Computer

For this method, you determine the ASF corrections to be applied by consulting the tables. The offsets may then be applied to the TDs displayed on the receiver readout or to the TDs of a destination waypoint obtained by interpolating between LOPs on an updated Loran chart. The TD offsets are entered directly into the computer as ASF corrections to the displayed TDs, thereby "uncorrecting" TDs *before* the conversion to lat/long is made. Once the offsets have been used to adjust the TDs, the resulting time differences are used by the computer to calculate lat/long. The resulting lat/long coordinates should agree almost precisely with the position plotted from the TDs.

To illustrate how ASF corrections are obtained from the tables and applied, assume your receiver is displaying a TD of 14308.3 on the 7980-W secondary and 44908.5 on the 7980-Y station. Checking your NOAA chart, you find these TDs put you approximately at latitude 28° 47.8′ North, longitude 83° 33.9′ West. Entering the 7980-W correction table (Figure 61) for these coordinates, you find the correction to be –0.2 microsecond. Subtracting the correction from the "W" TD gives a corrected TD of 14308.1

$$
\begin{array}{lll}
\text{Displayed TD} & = & 14308.3 \text{ ms} \\
\text{Correction} & = & -0.2 \text{ ms} \\
\hline
\text{Corrected TD} & = & 14308.1 \text{ ms}
\end{array}
$$

The correction obtained from the 7980-Y table (Figure 62) is –0.1 microsecond. Subtracting this value from the "Y" TD gives a corrected TD of 44908.4:

$$
\begin{aligned}
\text{Displayed TD} &= 44908.5 \text{ ms} \\
\text{Correction} &= -0.1 \text{ ms} \\
\hline
\text{Corrected TD} &= 44908.4 \text{ ms}
\end{aligned}
$$

These corrected TDs are now entered into the computer, and the computer will convert them to lat/long. The resulting geodetic fix will be very close to the fix you get plotting the original 14308.3/44908.5 LOPs on an updated Loran-C chart.

If the signal from a secondary transmitter is slowed by land path effects, the resulting TD will be greater than that of the idealized signal; ASF corrections then must be subtracted from the TD of the appropriate secondary. On the other hand, if the signal from the master transmitter is slowed, the TD will be less, and corrections must then be added to the TDs of both secondaries.

Consult your operator's manual to determine how to enter the ASF corrections obtained from the tables into the computer. Remember that separate corrections must be applied to the TD from each secondary.

Some receivers require that TDs first be entered as a waypoint into waypoint memory. Only after recalling that waypoint can the offsets be entered. In such an instance, select for storage the first (lowest numbered) address in waypoint memory.

ASF corrections will only be used by the computer to make lat/long conversions, and will not affect the TDs being displayed on the readout. Remember that the corrections are only accurate within a limited geographic area, and it will be necessary to enter new corrections as you sail from one location to another. Consult the correction tables for the offsets to be used in the area in which you are operating.

Correcting Latitude and Longitude before Lat/Long Conversions

Another way of entering ASF corrections is to enter latitude/longitude into the computer when the vessel is at a known geographic location, such as, for example, your home dock, the end of a pier, or a daymarker (keep in mind that the Coast Guard doesn't guarantee that buoys and other floating aids to navigation are actually located at the precise spot shown on a NOAA chart). Determine the actual lat/long of your known position as precisely as possible from a large-scale NOAA chart, then compare this with the position displayed by the computer after it has made a lat/long conversion using the uncorrected TDs of your position. The difference in the two sets of coordinates indicates the amount of error that must be corrected for. Clear the computer's calculated lat/long coordinates and enter the true coordinates; the computer will calculate ASF corrections based on the differences, and these corrections will then be automatically applied to all future lat/long conversions.

Positions displayed using this method of automatic lat/long offset computation should be very accurate as long as the boat is within a radius of about 20 miles of the position at which the ASFs were calculated. If you range farther afield, you should either repeat the process or consult the ASF correction tables for the appropriate offsets. When sailing close along the coast, especially if you are receiving transmitters located very near shore, the *percentage* of land path versus sea path that a signal travels can vary greatly as the boat moves only a short distance. Position accuracies, therefore, may be in greater error than those offshore.

Manually Entering Lat/Long Corrections

Some Loran receivers cannot automatically calculate offsets for you, so you must make the corrections manually. To do so, follow the procedure described above to determine the amount of correction to be applied: display the lat/long of your present position at a known location by pressing the LAT/LONG key, compare the displayed coordinates with the known coordinates, and determine the required correction by subtracting one from the other.

Let's say, for example, that the known coordinates of your position at your home dock are latitude 28° 35.4' North, longitude 82° 14.8' West. The computer displays the converted lat/long for this position as latitude 28° 36.9' North, longitude 82° 13.1' West. Find the difference between the two:

Displayed latitude = 28° 36.9'
−Known latitude   = 28° 35.4'
_____

Latitude correction =   −1.5'

The displayed latitude is greater than your known latitude, and you wish to change the displayed value to the known value; therefore, you must subtract 1.5' from the displayed latitude, and the offset for latitude is −1.5'.

Known longitude   = 82° 14.8'
−Displayed longitude = 82° 13.1'
_____

Longitude correction =   +1.7'

The true longitude is greater than the displayed value; since you wish to change the displayed value to agree with your true longitude, a +1.7' offset must be added to the displayed longitude.

Once the corrections are known, apply them to the displayed lat/long. Consult your operator's manual for the specific keystrokes to enter ASF corrections manually; in general, however, the offset for latitude is entered first, followed by the longitude correction.

Regardless of which method you use to enter ASF corrections, you should write the offsets down, since once the offsets are known, they can be entered again should you return to the same operating area, which is convenient if you don't happen to be near a known geographic landmark that can be used to determine your actual lat/long. Many receivers will store computed offsets and retain them even if the set is turned off, but this is not universally true.

Recalling Offsets Already in the Computer

Most receivers will warn you that TD offsets are entered in the computer and are being used when lat/long conversions are made by displaying a symbol on the readout. Should you wish to know what offsets are entered, you can find out by following the procedure described in your operator's manual.

CONVERTING LAT/LONG TO TDS

The navigation computer is able to convert latitude/longitude coordinates to corresponding time differences in much the same way that TDs are converted to lat/long. In this case, however, lat/long coordinates are first displayed manually on the readout, and the computer is then asked to make the conversion.

USING THE MOST ACCURATE ASF CORRECTIONS

When you require maximum accuracy from Loran (as you might when sailing along a rocky coast, negotiating a narrow channel, or operating in a crowded harbor), you should determine the *actual* ASFs for your operating area by direct measurement rather than depending on the theoretical (and possibly out-of-date) values that have been used to correct the chart LOPs or the ASF corrections programmed into your receiver. Plotted positions should then agree closely with actual positions, and waypoint navigation should be very accurate. If you use a waypoint frequently, as for example the seabuoy marking the entrance to your home channel, it's a good idea to come alongside periodically and check the current TDs. By "fine tuning" correction values in this fashion, *whether or not your receiver is capable of applying ASF corrections automatically*, you assure yourself of the highest possible level of accuracy. New-generation receivers will, with a little prompting from the navigator, calculate the precise ASFs at a particular location and apply them to subsequent lat/long conversions automatically, as described in the section, "Correcting Latitudes and Longitudes before Lat/Long Conversions." A resultant position accuracy of 50 to 100 feet is often obtained.

MANUALLY FORCING A TD PAIR

Having visited an area, and having once calculated the necessary local TD offsets for a secondary pair and stored them in the computer, you may return in the future and wish to use those offsets again. Remember, however, that those offsets are valid only for the specific secondary pair you were using on the first visit, and they cannot be used to correct another secondary pair. Because the receiver will automatically select a secondary pair on the basis of signal strength, gradient, and crossing angle, you should make certain that the stations the receiver is tracking are the same pair used before. If another secondary pair is being tracked, it will be necessary to *force* the receiver to track the original secondaries.

"Forcing a secondary pair" means that you disable the automatic station selection capability of the receiver and substitute stations that you select manually. Once the receiver is tracking these stations, you can apply the previously entered TD offsets and be assured that lat/long conversions are accurate. The procedure for forcing a secondary pair is detailed in Chapter 8, in which we discussed how to change secondaries when operating in the vicinity of a base line extension.

17 | Fringe Area Operations

In our earlier discussion of signal-to-noise ratios, cycle clips, and other signal characteristics, we have seen that there are times when a Loran-C receiver may have difficulty acquiring a signal and tracking it properly. These conditions of poor reception and unreliable tracking most frequently occur on the fringes of the area covered by a Loran-C chain. Must you stop using Loran under these conditions? Perhaps—although there is much that you, the operator, can do to improve reception and extend the range of Loran-C well beyond its normal limits. In this chapter, we will discuss the use of Loran when reception is poor and when operating in fringe areas. By understanding the concepts and practicing the procedures outlined here, you will be able to greatly enlarge the geographic area in which Loran-C can be relied upon for accurate navigation.

Most present-generation receivers normally operate on *automatic cycle selection*, in which the receiver automatically locks onto and tracks a pulse at the 30-microsecond point. Most receivers also feature *automatic station selection*, whereby the SNRs of all available stations in the chain are analyzed, and those stations with the highest SNRs are tracked. Automatic station selection works well in that part of the coverage area having strong signals; the farther you travel outside this area, however, the greater the probability of error due to weakening signal strength and poor station geometry.

In order to continue using Loran at extended range or in poor reception conditions, you may need to disengage the automatic tracking functions of the receiver and take control of station selection and tracking manually. To do so without introducing significant position errors, however, requires that you understand the fundamentals of Loran navigation well, know how to use the manual station selection and manual cycle control functions of the receiver, and use sound judgment.

HOW DO YOU KNOW YOU ARE IN A "FRINGE AREA?"

The term "fringe area," designating an area of poor Loran reception, is, unfortunately, somewhat nebulous. Reception quality at any point within the coverage area depends on a number of factors, many of which we have already alluded to: distance to the individual transmitters, sensitivity of the receiver, prevailing weather conditions, how the Loran antenna was installed and grounded, etc. In general, you can anticipate entering a "fringe area" as your boat approaches the approximate geographic limits of coverage of the chain being used as shown in the charts of Loran-C chains in the Appendix.

On the other hand, the best indication that you are nearing the limits of reliable reception is when your Loran receiver begins having difficulty acquiring and tracking one or more stations. Practically speaking, you are in a fringe area when your receiver can just barely track a master and two secondaries. (Rarely can you track three secondaries at extended range.) Specific indications of fringe area operations are:

- The signal-to-noise ratio of one or more of the secondaries will be marginal, causing the receiver to display a low SNR warning by flashing the TDs or latitude/longitude numbers on the display.

- The receiver may have difficulty tracking the signal of one or more stations on the third cycle, and will display a cycle-select alarm.

- The TDs or lat/long displayed are not the same as those of your actual position—an indication of cycle slip.

In general, any difficulty in acquiring and tracking signals, whatever the cause, should alert you to the possibility of being in an area of poor reception. Under these circumstances, you may find it necessary to take manual control of the receiver. Before doing so, however, make sure the receiver has had sufficient time to "settle," or lock onto the selected stations, subsequent to being turned on. Settling time varies from receiver to receiver and with signal strength; at great distances from the transmitter, and at lower signal strengths, the receiver may require a considerable time to settle down before the numbers on the display stop flashing. Typical settling times range from a couple of minutes when you are near a station to fifteen minutes or more on the fringes.

MANUAL STATION SELECTION

A Loran-C receiver operating in the automatic station selection mode selects the chain and secondaries to be used based on the criteria we discussed earlier: signal strength, gradient, and the crossing angle of LOPs. After selecting stations and starting to track them, the receiver will periodically (typically every five minutes or so) check the boat's present position and analyze whether or not to change chains or stations to obtain better geometry. As long as the receiver is left in the automatic mode, chain and station selection remain automatic, and the stations selected by the receiver will be the best for reliable reception and accurate navigation. Under certain conditions, however, such as fringe area operation, it may be necessary or desirable to turn off the automatic functions and take over control of station selection manually.

Where the receiver will automatically change chains or secondaries as you move from one coverage area to another, you may wish for some reason to continue receiving a certain chain or secondary. You can do this by overriding the automatic station select function; the receiver will remain on the stations you chose until you either re-engage the automatic functions or manually select other transmitters.

MANUAL CYCLE CONTROL

A part of the automatic functioning of a receiver is automatic cycle selection, by which the receiver automatically identifies the third cycle of an incoming pulse, locking on and tracking at that point. If the signal is weak or masked by strong interference, the receiver may have trouble finding the correct cycle; it may then lock onto a point 10 microseconds earlier or later than the third cycle, a condition called "cycle slip" (Figure 30). Although the receiver will continue to make time difference measurements as accurately as ever, the vessel's present position indicated by the TDs will be in error (the magnitude of the position error, as we have seen, depends on the gradient and crossing angle). In such a case, reception and position accuracy can be improved using manual cycle control.

Manual cycle control can be used to accomplish one of two different results:

- When a cycle slip problem has occurred, the TDs displayed on the receiver readout can be adjusted to agree with known time differences by manually shifting the tracking point.

- When operating at extended ranges or when interference is particularly strong, the strength of the incoming signal can be boosted by shifting the tracking point deeper (later) into the pulse.

Manual cycle control can be used in one of three different ways:

- You can disengage the automatic cycle selection function only.

- You can disengage automatic cycle selection and cycle step one or both secondaries.

- You can disengage the automatic cycle selection and cycle step the master and secondaries.

Let's look at each of these procedures separately.

Disengaging "Automatic Cycle Selection" Only

Using this procedure, you are merely bypassing the receiver's automatic selection of the third cycle on the incoming pulse to ensure that tracking continues on the correct cycle if reception deteriorates. Before disengaging the automatic mode, however, you must first determine the TDs or lat/long of your present position. After disengaging automatic cycle selection, check the TDs or lat/long displayed on the receiver readout against the known time difference values at your present position. If the readings agree with one another, and there are no flashing numbers on the display, you can continue to navigate with Loran. Lat/long conversions and other navigational functions will now be calculated from correct time differences.

Auto cycle select should be disengaged *only* when you must be absolutely certain that the receiver is tracking on the correct cycle, and it will generally not be necessary to do so when operating well within the normal limits of the Loran-C coastal coverage area.

Disengaging "Auto Cycle Select" and Cycle Stepping One or Both Secondaries

Cycle stepping one or both of the secondary transmitters is done when a cycle slip condition exists on the stations due to weak signal strength, etc., and you wish to step the tracking point back to the third pulse and bring the displayed TDs into agreement with the TDs or lat/long of your known present position. Again, this is done mainly to provide the correct time differences for the navigation computer to use in making its calculations of range and bearing, lat/long conversions, etc.

Let's assume that you are operating in a fringe area or in an area where Loran-C coverage is notoriously poor (in the lower reaches of the Bahamas, for example), and you know that reception may be unreliable. You have turned on the receiver and waited 15 to 20 minutes for the display to settle down, but the TDs and lat/long are still flashing, indicating a low SNR, cycle slip, or both. In this situation, you may be able to significantly improve reception by manually cycle stepping the secondary or secondaries that display incorrect TDs, until the TDs agree with those of your known position. (Naturally, since the receiver can no longer automatically select the two secondaries that are best suited for navigation, you'll want to make certain that you are using the correct stations; if necessary, review the discussion in Chapter 8 on the criteria for selecting stations.)

Here is the general series of steps you would take to control cycle selection manually and to cycle step the point at which the receiver is sampling the incoming pulse from a secondary:

- First, lock out automatic cycle selection. This is necessary so that, as you start manually changing the sampling point, the receiver does not sense that an incorrect cycle is being tracked and try to override manual adjustments.

- Next, check the TDs displayed against the known TDs of your present position. (Again, it's *imperative* that you know your actual position before using manual cycle selection. Determine the TDs from a large scale Loran-C overprinted chart, interpolating as carefully as possible.) Commonly, the TDs of the weakest station will disagree by plus or minus 10 microseconds, or one full cycle (although it could be off by 20 ms, 30 ms, or some other multiple of 10 ms). For example, instead of getting a TD of 45239.4 (your actual TD), the display may read 45249.4; in this case, the receiver is incorrectly tracking the *fourth* (40 ms) pulse instead of the third.

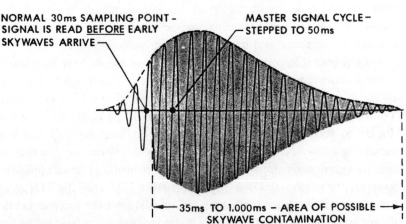

NORMAL 30ms SAMPLING POINT –
SIGNAL IS READ <u>BEFORE</u> EARLY
SKYWAVES ARRIVE

MASTER SIGNAL CYCLE –
STEPPED TO 50ms

35ms TO 1,000ms – AREA OF POSSIBLE
SKYWAVE CONTAMINATION

Figure 63 | Cycle stepping the tracking point on the master signal to a point later in the pulse increases signal strength, improving reception reliability in fringe areas, but also makes the signal vulnerable to sky-wave contamination.

- Now, change the incorrect TD to the correct values; cycle step up or down as appropriate until the correct TD appears on the display.

- Having cycle stepped one secondary so that the receiver is now tracking it on the correct cycle, repeat the procedure to cycle step the other secondary if necessary.

The receiver is now tracking on the correct cycle on both secondary pulses, and displays correct TDs and lat/long coordinates for your known present position. As long as the display doesn't flash (indicating even lower SNRs) you can continue to navigate. By cycle stepping the secondaries you have effectively extended the usable range of Loran-C well into a fringe area.

Disengaging "Auto Cycle Select" and Cycle Stepping Master and Secondaries

There may be times when, even though you have disengaged auto cycle select and used the cycle stepping procedure described above to improve reception of the secondaries, reception is still so poor that the TDs and lat/long flash often or continuously. In such circumstances, it may be possible to extend the range of Loran-C even farther by increasing the signal strength of the incoming pulses from each station. Although it isn't possible to increase transmission power, you can effectively do the same thing by reading the signal at a point on the pulse at which signal energy is higher than it is at the normal 30 ms tracking point. This is done by cycle stepping the sampling point deeper into the pulse.

You'll remember that, in our discussion of pulse characteristics in Chapter 6, we found that the radio energy (signal strength) of a Loran-C pulse rises rapidly shortly after the pulse is received, reaches a maximum signal strength early in the pulse, and then slowly diminishes. Since signal energy increases deeper into the pulse from the normal 30 ms sampling point (Figure 63), by shifting this point several cycles farther into the pulse you can increase the signal strength available to the receiver, thereby making it easier to read the signal above background noise (which in fringe areas can be quite strong). The chances of successfully acquiring and tracking the signal are considerably improved.

By stepping the tracking point of all *three* stations being received—the master and both secondaries—by the same amount, signal strength is increased without changing time differences.

The procedures for cycle stepping the master are essentially the same as those described above for cycle stepping secondaries. Let's summarize them:

- First, turn on the receiver and give it sufficient time to settle and acquire the master and secondaries, if it's going to.

- Determine the TDs or lat/long coordinates of your present position as accurately as possible.

- Select the best stations within the chain to use for navigation.

- Lock out auto cycle select so the receiver doesn't try to shift the tracking point as soon as you cycle-step it.

- Select the master station on the receiver.

- Cycle-step the tracking point on the master signal one or two cycles deeper into the pulse.

- Finally, cycle-step each of the secondary pulses the same amount, or until the TDs or lat/long agree with your present position.

You can now, once again, use Loran for navigation, but stay on the lookout for a flashing display warning of low SNRs.

Advancing the tracking point one 10 ms cycle into the pulse nearly *doubles* signal strength; advancing two cycles nearly triples it. You can easily verify this for yourself, and ascertain the strength of the signals on all three stations, by switching to the SNR function on the receiver. For a better idea of how signal strength changes as the tracking point is stepped, let's look more closely at how SNR changes as the tracking point is shifted.

In Figure 64, the sampling point is shown at four different points on a secondary pulse. At the 20 ms point, the SNR is 180. At this point, one cycle before the normal 30 ms sampling point, signal strength is still quite low. At the 30 ms point, the SNR is 300. This is the normal sampling point, but still the signal strength is too low for reliable tracking, leading to possible cycle slip—especially if the background noise level is high.

At the 100 ms point, the SNR is 540. At this point, about 70 ms deeper into the pulse than the normal sampling point, the signal strength reaches a maximum and is strong enough to be tracked. The SNR in this example is thus greatest with the tracking point stepped about seven cycles deeper into the pulse.

At the 200 ms point, the SNR is 220. Signal strength is declining again.

How far you step into the signal depends on the signal strength and reliability after each single cycle step is accomplished. If the signal is reliable (the TDs and lat/long don't flash) after advancing one cycle, it probably isn't necessary or desirable to advance any more. In order to retain reception as you travel deeper into a fringe area, you will likely have to step the tracking point even deeper into the master pulse; this will be obvious, however, when the display starts flashing again.

When you cycle-step deeper into a *secondary* signal, the time difference (TD) of that station *increases* at the rate of 10 ms per cycle; in other words, if you manually step from the third to the sixth cycle, the TD will become larger in value by 30 ms. Shifting the tracking point farther into

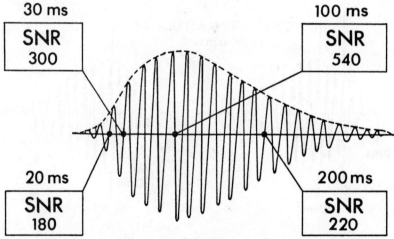

Figure 64 | SNR varies as the tracking point on the pulse changes: it becomes lower preceding the normal sampling point, reaches a maximum about one-third into the pulse, and decreases again even deeper into the pulse.

the pulse increases the interval between the time that the master signal is read and the time the secondary signal is read (Figure 65). Conversely, when the tracking point of the *master* is stepped deeper into the pulse, TDs will *decrease*. Stepping all transmitters up the same amount doesn't change time differences.

If your boat's position subsequently changes appreciably from the position at which you undertook cycle-stepping procedures, it's a good idea to check periodically to see whether the receiver is able once again to reliably acquire and track signals on its own.

A word of caution: Bear in mind that the normal 30 microsecond sampling point was chosen because it allows tracking before early arriving skywaves can contaminate the signal; moving deeper into the pulse makes the signal significantly more vulnerable to skywave interference (Figure 63). In spite of the possibility of skywave-induced errors, however, if the choice is between no Loran or a possible minor position error, you may decide to opt for degraded accuracy. You

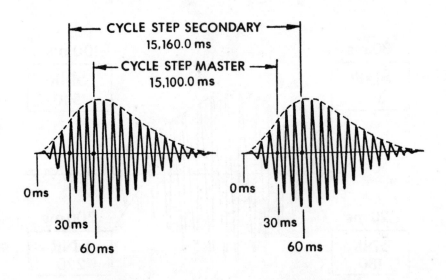

Figure 65 | TDs increase as the tracking point is stepped deeper into a secondary pulse, but decrease when stepped deeper into a master pulse.

should, however, use positions obtained from a cycle-stepped receiver with some degree of caution.

Also, remember that the accuracy of a Loran fix varies with your location relative to the stations being used. The farther you are from a station, the larger the gradient, and the greater the position error represented by each one-tenth microsecond error in TDs. When you are far enough from a station to be in a fringe reception area, the gradient is likely to be quite large, and errors can be great. When cycle slip occurs, a 10 ms shift in the tracking point represents at least a 1 nautical mile in position error, and the error can be much greater.

SUMMARY

By disengaging the receiver's automatic cycle selection function and manually controlling both the tracking point and signal strength of incoming signals, it's possible to extend the usable range of Loran-C well beyond the limits of the normal coverage area. Some people, in fact, report being able to use Loran in areas where there is not supposed to be *any* coverage at all. To do so, however, requires that you understand the nature of Loran signals and how the cycle-stepping methods described above affect both reception reliability and position accuracy.

After all this discussion of using Loran-C effectively in fringe areas, you may want to know where the most common fringe areas are located. As noted at the beginning of this chapter, you are in a fringe area anytime you are operating near the limits of Loran coverage as shown on coverage diagrams; it is possible to use Loran well beyond these limits with the cycle-stepping procedure just discussed.

Some popular cruising areas, however, have notoriously poor reception, and some degree of caution in using Loran should be exercised when sailing in these regions. Many people, for example, place the Bahamas near the top of their list of places to cruise, and are often disappointed to discover that Loran-C coverage is only good around Grand Bahama Island and the Abacos in the northern part of the island chain; southward from Andros and the northern end of Eleuthera, reception becomes increasingly unreliable.

Crews bound for Bermuda likewise find that reliable reception peters out before they arrive. This lovely group of islands is unfortunately situated outside the normal coverage areas of either the Northeast or Southeast United States chains.

The entire Gulf of Mexico is well covered by the Southeast chain, except for the western part of the Bay of Campeche from about Brownsville, Texas to Campeche, Mexico. It should be noted, however, that some Loran users have complained of poor accuracy in two areas of the Gulf. LOP crossing angles along the southeast coast of Florida, from the Y baseline extension at Jupiter to Key West, are shallow, and position accuracies are often less than desirable. Likewise, in the western Gulf from Galveston southward, navigators using the W and X stations, which provide the best signal strength, have complained of shallow crossing angles.

A popular cruising area on the U.S. West Coast is along the Baja Peninsula; folks sailing there often find themselves navigating by piloting or RDF, however, since Loran-C coverage from the West Coast (9940) chain ends around San Diego, and there is, unfortunately, no Mexican chain to provide coverage farther south. In fact, Loran-C coverage of the entire U.S. West Coast is less accurate than for other coastal areas. This is due primarily to the wide variety of coastal terrain (including mountains, rain forests, deserts, etc.) and the resulting difficulty of accurately determining ASF corrections for the area. Calibration of West Coast charts is a priority of the National Ocean Service, and their accuracy should improve measurably in the future. Due to the lack of adequate survey data, charts of the entrance to Puget Sound and the Straits of Juan de Fuca are presently without any Loran LOPs whatever.

Although reception is adequate, Loran navigation on Lake Superior, Lake Erie, and Lake Ontario is less accurate than in many areas due to inaccuracies in Loran charts resulting from a paucity of field data, and to seasonal variations in signal propagation. As more field measurements are made, the charts will improve.

Finally, although of little interest to mariners, the entire mid-continental stretch of the United States is devoid of Loran coverage, which is an aggravation for the increasing number of aircraft pilots who are making greater navigational use of the system than ever before.

18 | Skywave Navigation

In Chapter 6 we discussed skywaves, a skywave being that part of a Loran-C radio signal that propagates upward, bounces off the ionosphere, and is received sometime after its companion groundwave (Figure 15). Because the groundwave takes a more direct path from the transmitter to your boat, its time of travel is a truer measure of your distance from a transmitter, and thus groundwave reception is preferred over skywave reception.

A groundwave's signal is strong near the transmitting station but is rapidly attenuated by interference from surface friction and objects it encounters en route. By the time it reaches your position, it may be very weak, especially if your boat is a great distance from the transmitter. The skywave, on the other hand, loses little energy propagating through clear air and is often much stronger upon arrival at your boat than its companion groundwave.

If you are operating at great distances (1,500 miles or more) from a transmitter, or if there is considerable weather-related interference, the SNR of the groundwave may be very low, and your Loran receiver may have a difficult time acquiring and tracking the signal without cycle slip. In these conditions, it is possible to use the stronger skywave signal for Loran navigation.

Skywave navigation is at best very tricky and should be used as a last resort. When using skywaves, the time differences displayed may be in error by many microseconds, causing position errors as great as ten miles or more. Navigating with skywaves is a technique usually reserved for use when well offshore, considerably beyond the normal limits of a Loran-C coverage area; when operating in deep water and with few navigational hazards, some degree of position inaccuracy can be tolerated. Positions obtained from skywaves should be carefully verified with all other means at hand before being used for accurate position finding in areas where hazards to navigation are present.

DETERMINING WHICH SIGNALS ARE SKYWAVES

Since skywaves have very strong SNRs, much stronger than those of groundwaves (unless you are operating near a transmitter), an analysis of the signal strength of the signal from each transmitter being tracked will indicate if any of the incoming signals are in reality skywaves. Additionally, some receivers will indicate that some signals are suspected of being skywaves by displaying some form of warning, such as "SKY," on the readout.

CORRECTIONS FOR SKYWAVE RECEPTION

Once you have determined which signals are skywaves, you must ascertain the correction to be applied. The Defense Mapping Agency publishes large-area Loran-C plotting charts, which include skywave navigation information. Corrections are provided for specific GRIs and transmitters in much the same fashion that ASF corrections are listed according to the chain and secondaries being tracked. For example, skywave corrections look like this:

$$9960W \quad +02D \quad GS \quad -28D$$
$$9960W \quad -05N \quad GS \quad -36N$$

The 9960W +02 means that when using the 9960 Northeast U.S. chain, if *both* the master and the W secondary are being received as skywaves, a 0.2 microsecond correction must be added to the time difference of the W station if the signal is received during the daytime (D); nighttime skywave signals (N) require subtraction of a 0.5 microsecond correction using those stations.

The GS –28D means that during the daytime, if the master signal is a groundwave (G) and the W secondary is a skywave (S), 28 microseconds must be subtracted from the TD of the W secondary. A similar situation during nighttime reception would require that 36 microseconds be subtracted.

CALCULATING POSITION WITH SKYWAVES

Having determined the applicable corrections from the chart, add or subtract them to the displayed time differences using the procedure for applying ASF correction discussed in Chapter 16. The computer can then convert the corrected time differences to lat/long using the method described in that chapter.

As with ASF corrections, it is helpful in skywave navigation to know your position with some degree of certainty. A prudent navigator will also use other methods of position finding in conjunction with Loran-C under such conditions of poor reception.

19 | Ambiguous Positions

As we have seen, Loran-C LOPs are hyperbolically curved lines, and a Loran fix is the point where two such lines intersect. Because of their hyperbolic shapes, however, two Loran LOPs will often cross at two different points on the earth's surface; your position might then be at one of two intersections, either of which would satisfy the criteria for a fix from the point of view of your receiver. In other words, your position would be ambiguous (Figure 66). Obviously, only *one* of the points would be your actual position—but which one?

Ambiguous, or complementary, positions are most likely to occur when only two secondaries and the master are being received, and you are operating very near the baseline extension of a master/secondary pair or a secondary/secondary pair. In this situation, if your receiver is operating in the "automatic tracking" mode, it could choose the wrong intersection as your fix and display incorrect coordinates. Many receivers will flash a warning such as "AMBIG" when this occurs. If your receiver doesn't warn you, you may only become aware of the potential problem through close inspection of the points of intersection of printed Loran LOPs. When ambiguity exists, you will have to decide which coordinates represent your boat's actual location.

Although the procedure for resolving position ambiguity varies with the receiver, it generally involves analyzing the lat/long coordinates of both positions and comparing each with where you think you are. Generally, the two positions are so far apart that it is relatively easy to choose the right one. As a conscientious navigator, you don't rely on any one aid to navigation; rather, you maintain an updated plot of your dead-reckoning position, which you cross-check with Loran fixes and other navigational information obtained from compass bearings on identifiable objects ashore, SatNav fixes, RDF bearings, and so on. As a result, you can usually define your position within a mile or two, at worst. If one of the two possible fixes based on intersecting LOPs is very near where you think you are, the other is probably quite some distance away. It's reasonable, then, to select the point of intersection closest to your DR position, dismissing the other solution as a fluke of geometry. Once the correct position has been established, bring its coordinates up on the readout; the receiver will then automatically track as the true position the lat/long coordinates that were last displayed.

If you can't readily clarify your position through dead reckoning, use your Loran receiver to help resolve the ambiguity. If you can receive a third secondary station, switch to it, so that your receiver is tracking the new station and one of the original secondaries. The lat/long coordinates of this position should closely agree with one of the two ambiguous positions, thereby indicating which is correct. Again, call up the correct coordinates on the readout, and the receiver will track them automatically.

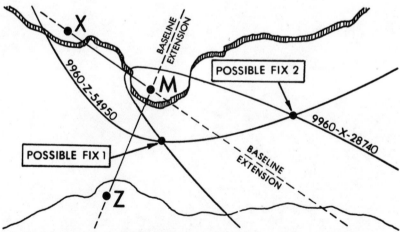

Figure 66 | Two hyperbolically curving LOPs that define your present position will often cross at two points on the earth's surface, but *which* one of these intersections represents your true position is ambiguous.

Even after the receiver has begun tracking the proper solution, it can be thrown off should you later cross a baseline extension. There are positions on either side of the baseline extension that bear the same time differences, and these points are indistinguishable in the receiver. Therefore, the position you chose earlier as your actual position may not be successfully tracked across the baseline extension, and as you leave the vicinity of the baseline extension you may once again find it necessary to choose between two possible positions.

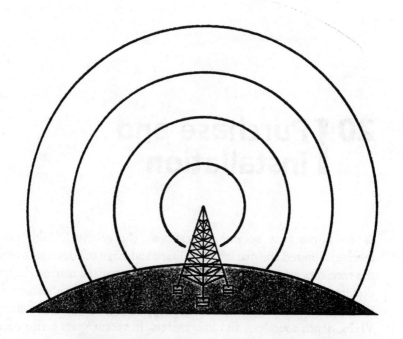

SECTION FOUR

Installation and Interference Reduction

20 | Purchase and Installation

When Loran first became operational, the relatively high price of receivers limited the market to military and large commercial users, and the receivers were available only through specialized marine electronics dealers. As prices dropped, however, yachtsmen and fishermen found Loran attractive, and receivers began appearing in chandleries alongside VHFs, depth sounders, and knotmeters. In recent years mail-order and discount outlets have also begun offering Loran receivers for sale. What are the pros and cons of buying from these various sources?

Purchasing your receiver from a dealer specializing in the sales, installation, and servicing of marine electronics often means paying more. Because their reputations depend on customer satisfaction, however, these firms generally provide expert installations, post-installation troubleshooting, prompt after-sale service, and the benefit of the dealer's guarantee as well as the manufacturer's warranty. If the unit is defective, the dealer will repair or replace it. This usually is the hassle-free way to buy and install Loran.

The price of the same receiver purchased from a chandlery or mail-order house (particularly the latter) is often substantially less, making this an attractive alternative to the cost-conscious buyer. Bear in mind, however, that since you aren't paying for installation, once you get the receiver home (or receive it in the mail), *you* must install it and get it working. Although the operator's manual provides installation instruc-

156

tions, *you* decide where to put the receiver, position the antenna for best reception, and run the power and ground wiring; *you* perform installation evaluations, analyze signal strengths, look for sources of interference, and find ways to filter noise. And if the unit doesn't perform up to expectation, it's up to *you* to figure out why.

Many new Loran owners have successfully completed their own installations, learning much about Loran in the process, and found themselves better able to troubleshoot problems that arise later. If you don't feel qualified to complete the installation yourself, however, you might look for help. A chandlery or mail-order house can't be expected to provide technical assistance, so you may find it necessary to hire an electronics technician to help site the antenna, select an adequate ground, analyze the causes of interference, or determine ways to suppress noise. Obviously, this adds to the cost of the unit, often making it at least as expensive as the same receiver purchased from a marine electronics dealer in the first place. Non-specialty outlets generally don't have the facilities or expertise to repair defective units, so if your receiver malfunctions you will have to ship it to the manufacturer for servicing.

Finally, there is the question of calibration of notch filters. Many manufacturers claim that before it leaves the factory a receiver's preset notch filters are tuned to filter out noise from known interference sources along both the East and West coasts of the U.S., and that no additional calibration of the filters is necessary before a receiver is installed. Some dealers, disagree, however, claiming that filters are not always properly tuned at the factory, and to ensure optimum reception should be checked and calibrated before installation. Most marine electronics dealers check notch filter settings before installing a unit; this is never done when a unit is purchased through a chandlery or discount supplier. If you suspect your filters need adjusting, take your receiver to an electronics dealer; if you didn't buy your Loran from him, the dealer will charge you for the service.

The choice is to pay a higher price and get a complete, guaranteed installation, or to buy at a discount and do the work yourself. The decision is easier if you are aware of the benefits and pitfalls of each alternative, and if you first carefully analyze your own abilities: how handy you are with tools, your own level of electronic expertise, and the depth of your pockets. Regardless of your choice, the following section will give you an overview of the installation process.

INSTALLATION

A Loran-C receiver is a precision instrument, capable of providing a variety of extremely accurate and reliable navigational data. This high level of performance can only be achieved, however, if the receiver is installed properly, and reliability can suffer greatly if installation guidelines are not followed. On the other hand, merely installing the receiver properly and then successfully acquiring signals at the dock is not a guarantee that the unit will give maximum performance at sea, where reception is affected by such factors as the operation of other shipboard electrical equipment, external interference, and weather.

The best test of the quality of an installation is signal strength, and it is prudent to perform a series of post-installation tests measuring SNRs. A summary of these tests is found at the end of this chapter.

Unpacking and Inspecting the Receiver

If you buy your receiver from a mail-order discount house, inspect it for obvious damage and ensure that all parts were shipped. These include the receiver itself, an antenna coupler, coaxial and power cables, connectors, a mounting yoke, and the operator's manual.

It's a good idea to retain the shipping carton and packing material in the event the unit must be returned to the manufacturer. Also, don't neglect to send in the warranty card; failure to fill it out properly and return it to the manufacturer generally voids the warranty.

Installation Considerations

Several factors contribute to a successful installation:

1. Initial placement of the receiver
2. Initial placement of the antenna

3. Selection of a power source
4. Provision of an adequate radio-frequency ground
5. Minimization of onboard radio-frequency interference
6. Conducting the preliminary performance evaluation
7. Final placement and installation of the receiver and antenna
8. Conducting a final performance evaluation

Receiver Placement

The location chosen for the Loran receiver is important in determining its operational longevity and its ease of use, the latter implying both ease of access to controls and ease of viewing. A popular location is at or near the boat's navigation station. Although it is highly desirable to locate the receiver where it can be seen by the person at the helm, it is often not practical to do so; in such situations, installing a course deviation indicator in the cockpit is an effective alternative.

When selecting a location, remember that electronic devices are easily damaged by the corrosive qualities of salt water, and although a Loran receiver's water-resistant housing is designed to protect it from light salt spray, the instrument may nonetheless be rendered completely inoperable if immersed in seawater.

Excessive heat from cabin heaters, stoves, and exhaust pipes can also damage delicate electronic circuits. In addition, the unit must be installed with adequate ventilation on all sides.

If the receiver utilizes a liquid-crystal display (LCD), prolonged exposure to direct sunlight may cause the numbers to fade or the entire display to turn dark and unreadable; the numbers will generally reappear, however, when the display cools. If the receiver is installed in the dash or console of a small boat, adding a smoked Plexiglas cover will help protect it from both sunlight and salt spray.

On small, high-speed boats, the receiver should be securely shock-mounted using rubber pads to protect it from excessive vibration. If mounted in "quick-disconnect" fashion using bolts with wing nuts, it can easily be removed from the boat for theft protection.

The best viewing angle for many receivers is from dead ahead to slightly above the front panel. Most can either be mounted on a flat surface or hung overhead on a mounting yoke. The location selected should provide sufficient room behind the unit for the routing of antenna, power, and ground cables.

To avoid possible deviation errors, install the receiver no closer than 2 feet from your ship's magnetic compass.

Before finalizing the location of the receiver, operate the unit for a period of time and conduct the preliminary performance evaluations detailed in the operator's manual. Final mounting of the unit should come only after you are fully satisfied with its performance.

Antenna and Coupler

The antenna and antenna coupler comprise an integral and important part of your receiver; indeed, their mounting location is perhaps the single most important factor affecting performance. An improperly installed antenna will prevent even the best receiver from operating reliably.

The antenna picks up incoming Loran signals, which are then amplified by a radio frequency amplifier in the coupler. The amplified signal is then sent to the receiver, where it is processed and displayed. Unamplified, the signal is too weak to be used by the receiver. The coupler is tuned to the receiver; if the antenna, coupler, or both are damaged, they should be replaced with the same type or another type recommended in the operator's manual.

Generally, Loran manufacturers recommend using 8-foot fiberglass whip-type antennas. Longer or shorter antennas have the wrong capacitance and may distort incoming signals, and stainless steel antennas, with their greater mass, may damage the coupler as the boat pitches or rolls. The antenna should have a chrome-plated brass base; antennas with steel bases corrode easily.

Most receivers are shipped with associated coaxial cables and an attached connector that plugs into the back of the receiver. The operator's manual will recommend maximum and minimum cable lengths, figures that should be kept in mind when finalizing the antenna mounting location

Antenna and Coupler Location

The best location for the antenna and coupler is as high on your boat as possible, with special care taken to locate them as far as possible from standing rigging, stays, shrouds, metal masts, and other antennas.

A Loran antenna has a conical 90-degree "cone of interference" within which incoming signals are received; this active area describes a 45-degree angle to the axis of the antenna. Stays, masts, and other metal objects protruding into this cone significantly weaken incoming Loran signals. In addition, "blind spots" within the reception area can occur when standing rigging of any kind is positioned between the antenna and the transmitting station.

Mounting the antenna in close proximity to medium- and high-frequency transmitting antennas, such as VHF-FM and SSB antennas, can cause interference due to direct inductive coupling between the transmitting antenna and the Loran receiving antenna. To minimize this effect, manufacturers recommend a minimum separation of 3 feet vertically and 6 feet horizontally between antennas. The antenna should also be mounted as far as practical from other possible interference sources such as televisions, color depth recorders, and engine alternators. If radar or radio direction-finding equipment is aboard, ensure that the Loran antenna is clear of the radar antenna turning circle and at least 6 feet from an RDF loop antenna.

For best reception, Loran antennas should be mounted vertically. Under certain conditions, however, it may be necessary to tilt one slightly; this is usually done to maximize SNR by reducing inductive coupling between the antenna and nearby transmitting antennas. The tilt should be minimal, and under no circumstances should it exceed 45 degrees.

The best antenna location on a sailboat is at the top of a mast; if a VHF antenna is already mounted there, a combination Loran/VHF antenna may be an option if one is compatible with your receiver. On sloops, cutters, and catboats, the preferred location is the top of the mainmast; on ketches and yawls, the top of the mizzenmast is the next best choice.

If you already have an "antenna farm" sprouting from your masthead, it may be necessary to mount the antenna on the stern pulpit rail, although this solution is precluded by an overhanging boom. Attach the coupler to a vertical stanchion with hose clamps, and mount the antenna on the extreme port or starboard side rather than in the center of the boat. Ensure that the coupler is *above* the rail on which it is mounted. By tilting the antenna slightly aft, it's easy to move the antenna's cone of interference beyond the backstay. Fiberglass antenna extensions, which are available in 4- and 8-foot lengths, can be used to move the coupler away from the backstay.

An insulated backstay may be used as an antenna, but this is not a preferred solution. The insulated length should be about 8 feet, and the coupler must be located very close to the lower end.

On powerboats, a good location is atop the flying bridge or on the top or side of the cabin. The most common location is on top of the wheelhouse. On center console boats, mount on the gunwale or on top of the console. The same rules apply as on sailboats: mount the antenna clear of any metallic objects, including other antennas, tuna towers, outriggers, etc., and keep the top of the coupler above any rail on which it is mounted.

Mounting the Antenna Coupler

The coupler is designed to be mounted on a fiberglass extension pole, a stanchion, or a swivel mount on the side of the deckhouse. The lower section has a 1"–14 thread mounting to mate with the pole or swivel mount. Before selecting the final location, analyze signal strength with the antenna mounted in various locations around the boat—then use the spot that provides the strongest SNR based on the preliminary evaluation.

Power Requirements

The nominal operating voltage of a Loran receiver is 12 volts DC; the usable voltage range is generally between 11 and 15 volts. Power consumption is very low, on the order of 1 to 4 amps. Most receivers require a negative-ground power source; if your boat has a positive ground or a floating ground, you'll find it necessary to use a power converter.

It's seldom necessary to provide a separate battery for the Loran, but if you do find this necessary, take care that the battery you use will not be switched off inadvertently, causing a loss of tracking. To prevent interference caused by RF energy feeding back into the Loran power circuit, don't connect the receiver's power leads to bus bars or other power sources that feed VHF, SSB, or other radio transmitters; rather, connect the Loran leads directly to the ship's batteries. Likewise, never connect the power leads directly to a boat's ignition system (a not uncommon practice in small powerboats with easily accessible ignition switches), since doing so almost guarantees unwanted interference. To further reduce the possibility of RF interference, route power leads as far as possible from other electrical cables.

When wiring the receiver to the power supply, it's important to check for proper polarity; reversed polarity can damage the receiver. Note that boat wiring does not follow the same wiring convention used in the household: on boats, the *black* wire is ground, and is therefore connected to the *negative* terminal. The *red* or *white* lead is connected to the *positive* terminal. If you accidentally connect the wiring backwards, the fuse in the back of the receiver will blow; replace it with another of the *same amperage* after the wiring error is corrected.

Direct current flowing in a wire creates an electromagnetic field that, if placed near a magnetic compass, can cause significant deviation in compass headings. This is particularly noticeable when positive and negative power leads are laid out parallel to each other, in which case each wire's electromagnetic field amplifies the other. The worst situation occurs when the positive lead is run on one side of the compass and the negative on the other. To reduce unwanted compass deviation from electrical wiring, route all power leads, including those for your Loran receiver, as far from the compass as possible (two feet is usually sufficient), and *twist* the positive and negative leads together; this causes the two magnetic fields to cancel each other.

Grounding Requirements

A good RF ground is essential to proper operation of Loran receivers. Proper grounding improves the signal-to-noise ratio, whereas a poor ground results in erratic operation of the receiver and the navigation computer. On steel-hulled boats, the hull itself affords an excellent ground; on wood or fiberglass vessels, it may be necessary to install a grounding plate on the hull beneath the waterline specifically for the purpose. The grounding plate should have a minimum size of 3 inches on a side. Lacking a grounding plate, the ground wire should be securely connected to the engine block. Although it *may* provide an acceptable ground, most Loran manufacturers suggest not using the negative terminal of the ship's battery.

The ground wire should be at least #18 gauge, and heavier is preferred. A 1-inch-wide braided copper strap is often used instead, but corrosion of the fine strands in the braid is a drawback. The Loran ground wire should never be used as a ground for any other onboard electrical equipment, and it should be kept as short as possible.

Normally, only the receiver itself is grounded; to minimize excessive interference, however, it may occasionally be necessary to ground the antenna coupler as well. The necessity for grounding the coupler can be ascertained by the inability to obtain usable SNRs during preliminary performance checks.

PRELIMINARY PERFORMANCE EVALUATION

After completing the initial installation, grounding, and power hookup of the receiver, you should undertake a series of tests to evaluate the unit's performance, so you can identify and correct any problems before finalizing the installation. These checks are simple but effective. Before beginning the evaluation, turn off all onboard electrical equipment, including the engine, and operate the receiver on ship's DC power.

Turn the receiver on and select a chain; once the receiver has settled down and all warning indicators are off, ensure that it is tracking the pulse on the correct cycle. Then switch to the SNR mode and scan the signal strengths of all available secondaries; select a station with a relatively *low* SNR and record that value. You'll use this reading as a reference for gauging the effect of various items of electrical equipment on signal quality.

Start the engine and run it up to cruising speed. Allow the receiver to settle, and see what happens to the SNR; record the reading. If your boat has two engines, repeat this step for each one. Then turn off the engine and turn on the generator; with the Loran operating on the boat's electrical system, again record any change in the SNR.

One by one, turn on each piece of electrical equipment and observe how its operation affects the SNR of the selected station. Be sure to check all equipment that runs on electricity: electronic gear, radar, VHF, SSB, bilge pumps, water pumps, incandescent and fluorescent lights, television, air conditioners, microwave oven, blender, refrigerator, windshield wiper motors, electric winches and windlasses, exhaust fans, autopilot—everything. If the SNR remains the same, or at worst shows a drop of only 10 to 15 percent, it is an indication that a particular piece of equipment is not producing significant RF interference; if the SNR drops noticeably, the item is seriously degrading Loran reception, and you must take steps to reduce interference from that source. Analyze each suspicious piece of equipment several times to ensure that any drop in SNR is real and is attributed to the correct source.

The electrical systems of many boats are shielded, and produce little interference; on such vessels you may never experience an SNR drop of more than 10 percent. On other vessels you may encounter several different power supplies, corroded DC motors powering bilge and pressure water pumps, overloaded circuits, and poor grounding systems; when electrical gear is switched on, you'll be lucky to receive *any* Loran signal above all the interference.

Be aware that SNRs are seldom rock-steady, and don't get too concerned if they fluctuate. That's normal—any electrical interference could cause it, and the culprit could be electrical and electronic gear outside your boat. Don't be too quick to damn your bilge pump for causing a low SNR; check the readings several times, and you might find the interference is coming from an external source instead. (For this reason, you'll find it advantageous to move the boat some distance from overhead power lines or bridges before starting the preliminary evaluation.)

This evaluation should also be used to verify that the location you've selected for the antenna and coupler is the best possible. Move the antenna to various locations around the boat, noting resultant changes in the SNR. You might also experiment with different routes for the power cables to minimize interference. Once you've found the best spot for the antenna, you can mount it permanently.

POST-INSTALLATION EVALUATION

After mounting the antenna and coupler at their final location, give the receiver one final checkout: turn on all the electrical equipment and see if you get acceptable SNRs with everything running. It's even a good idea at this point to back the boat out of her slip and power around at cruising speed, monitoring signal strengths all the while. Finally, to ensure that signal strength is maximized, you might repeat this entire procedure using several other secondary stations.

If the SNRs look good after all that, you've got an up-and-running, fully operational Loran-C receiver that should give you the full accuracy and reliability this marvelous instrument is capable of providing.

In Chapter 21 we'll look at the various kinds of onboard interference, and methods of suppressing them.

21 | Sources of Interference

Loran-C reception is highly susceptible to interference from radio-frequency radiation sources, whether those sources are aboard or external to your boat. "Noise" tends to overpower incoming signals, burying them in unwanted background clutter, and noise is particularly worrisome when you are operating at some distance from a transmitter and the Loran signal is weak to begin with.

There are many possible sources of electrical noise aboard a boat, and identifying them is often a time-consuming and frustrating task. It's an important one, though, and the possible improvements in reception justify the effort. A Loran receiver represents a substantial investment; don't let interference rob you of the quality you paid for. The post-installation evaluation described in Chapter 20 is designed to help determine signal quality and locate interference sources aboard your boat.

It was noted earlier that notch filters are installed in a receiver to filter out RF noise within specific frequency ranges. You might then ask, "Why must I try to reduce onboard interference? Don't the notch filters take care of it?" Unfortunately, no. Notch filters suppress noise generated by sources *outside* your boat, but do nothing to reduce interference from electrical equipment installed on board. To reduce onboard noise, you must first locate the source and then find some means of attenuating it.

The problem of onboard interference is getting worse, aggravated by several factors.:

- A steady increase in the amount of electrical or electronic equipment and associated wiring in a modern vessel

- An increase in the number of transmitting antennas associated with this equipment

- The current trend toward high power in transmitters

The most common sources of onboard interference are the following:

- Alternator noise from engine or generator alternators, most frequently at cruising rpms

- Voltage regulators

- Inverters on raster-scan radars and the power inverters used in strobe lights and other electronic gear

- Engine ignition systems on gasoline engines

- Late-model autopilots

- Single-sideband (SSB) radio, when transmitting

- Some wind speed indicators and knotmeters

- DC motors on bilge pumps and water pumps

- Windshield wiper motors

- Prop shafts

- Television sets

- Microwave ovens

- Refrigerators

- Fluorescent lighting

Alternator noise is the most frequent and strongest source, next in line being fluorescent lights and television sets. Each alone creates enough noise to affect Loran reception seriously, and suppression is mandatory if your receiver is to work properly.

Alternator Noise

Alternator noise comes from the engine or generator alternator, which is used for battery charging. Each time the diode bridge in the alternator shuts off—which occurs 1,000 to 5,000 times per second, depending on engine RPM—it radiates a very short high-energy pulse. Each pulse creates a "spike" of radio-wave interference that travels throughout the boat along the power wiring and radiates out into space. A Loran receiver picks up this RF noise and processes it as it would the Loran signal, which results in a very poor signal-to-noise ratio. This "spiking" increases with the current load, and this is exacerbated when the batteries are recharging immediately after starting the engine.

Alternator noise is suppressed by installing an appropriate filter at the output of each alternator. The usual specification for such a filter is a 10,000 or 20,000 microfarad, vented, electrolytic capacitor, 50-volt minimum working voltage, rated at 125 degrees Celsius. The capacitor is connected from the output (+) terminal of the alternator to the boat's grounding system, the alternator housing, or the engine block and is mounted as close to the alternator as possible. You may find it necessary to check SNRs to determine which ground produces maximum signal strength.

On occasion it may not be possible to filter alternator noise enough to allow proper Loran reception. In such cases, it may be necessary to rebuild the alternator or purchase a new one.

Voltage Regulator

The voltage regulator generates RF noise by applying a series of fast pulses to the field winding of the alternator. These pulses are switched on and off by a mechanical relay or by a solid-state regulator—that is, a transistor. The solid state regulator tends to be noisier than the mechanical relay.

Voltage regulator noise can be suppressed by installing a capacitor at the battery connection of the regulator, again using the shortest possible capacitor leads. The type of capacitor required must be determined by experimentation, depending on its effective series resistance (ESR). Try different capacitors with ESRs between about 100 and 5,000 microfarads, and use the one that best improves SNR. The assistance of a qualified marine electronics technician may be needed in suppressing noise from the voltage regulator.

Fluorescent Lights

Fluorescent lights operating off the ship's 12-volt DC power system generate both conducted and radiated RF noise, which is picked up and processed by a Loran receiver. Suppressing noise from these lights is difficult. Try installing a MAR-P5 filter (manufactured by Marine Technology of Long Beach, CA) or equivalent in the positive lead to each light, then bonding all parts of the metal chassis together to the negative power lead. Often, the best solution is simply to refrain from using fluorescent lights when navigating with Loran.

Television Sets and Color Depth Recorders

Television sets, especially inexpensive black-and-white models, and small computers both generate a great deal of RF interference, as may other devices, such as color depth recorders, that utilize television-like displays. No practical means of shielding this RF energy from a receiver has yet been devised. To circumvent the problem altogether, simply leave the TV and computers off when using Loran, particularly if you can't locate the Loran receiver far enough from these sources to alleviate noise.

Engine Ignition

Conventional gasoline engine ignition systems do not affect Loran-C, but certain types of electronic ignition systems containing DC-DC inverters may cause interference. Using resistor spark plugs *and* resistor plug cables may help the situation, and a filter capacitor installed in the positive lead from the ignition system to the ignition key will usually completely eliminate the problem.

Other common sources of RF interference include electronic devices that utilize digital displays, such as digital depth sounders, knotmeters, tachometers, and windspeed indicators. Such devices incorporate switching circuits that can introduce interference into the boat's electrical system. Try locating the Loran receiver some distance from these instruments.

Finally, installation of a powerline filter such as those available from Marine Technology will often alleviate interference from any of the above sources. If all efforts fail, turn to a Loran dealer or other qualified marine electronics technician for assistance.

Epilogue | The Future of Loran-C

Loran-A filled a critical navigational gap for military ships and aircraft during World War II, and Loran-C has become perhaps the most widely used navigation system of the 1970s and 1980s. Since Loran-C became operational, however, two new systems, Transit (SatNav) and the Global Positioning System (GPS), have come "on line." What, then, are the future prospects for Loran-C?

As of this writing, the U.S. Coast Guard, which administers and operates the Loran-C system, plans to divest itself of responsibility for all non–U.S. chains by 1992. Whether or not transmitters outside the United States will remain in operation after that time is uncertain, depending primarily on the commitment of the host country to assume operational and financial responsibility for the system.

Present plans call for all United States chains to remain in operation until the year 2000, although many experts believe the system will stay on line for an indefinite period beyond that. In the United States, Loran-C is used increasingly for aircraft navigation. As a result, the Coast Guard, in cooperation with the Federal Aviation Administration, is considering the addition of a new chain to fill the large midcontinental gap in coverage between the Great Lakes and West Coast chains. The new chain would benefit primarily aircraft navigation; its implementation depends largely on whether or not the Department of Transportation views the chain as being compatible with GPS. In addition, plans are underway to make the Port Clarence secondary transmitter (now a part of the 9990 North Pacific chain) a dual-rated station with the 7960 Gulf of Alaska chain, which will greatly expand Loran coverage for south central Alaska.

Other possible future areas of coverage include the Gulf of Tonkin and the west coast of Scandinavia, and countries such as Canada, France, Norway, Denmark, West Germany, Iceland, Saudi Arabia, Egypt, the Soviet Union, and China have expressed interest in either building or expanding Loran-C systems along their shores. This indicates that the system may remain operational throughout the globe for some time to come.

The Coast Guard is conducting tests on a "differential Loran" system intended for use at the approaches to, and within, selected harbors. By reducing the diurnal fluctuations in TDs caused by day and nighttime atmospheric variations, differential Loran reportedly would provide positional accuracies within 30 to 60 feet, thus enabling vessels to navigate precisely in constricted areas. The exact additional secondary factor (ASF) corrections for a particular harbor at a specific time would be determined by continual automatic monitoring of actual TDs at a known location, and these corrections would be broadcast to vessels operating in the approach and harbor areas. Although present plans call for ASF corrections to be broadcast via VHF radiotelephone, at some point transmission may be digitized, enabling Loran receivers to apply the corrections automatically. Although differential Loran is still in the conceptual stage, the fact that it is being considered at all underscores the probability of Loran-C remaining a viable system for years to come.

Yet another potential use for Loran-C lies in the area of land transportation. Concerted efforts are underway in both the United States and Japan to develop a navigation system based on Loran for use in automobiles and delivery vehicles.

TRANSIT (SATNAV)

Although Transit, the present six-satellite navigation system, has been in operation for over a decade, it is an unsuitable replacement for Loran, especially for the small-boat sailor. Loran-C is primarily a *coastal* navigation system, while Transit was designed as a global aid to *offshore* navigation. Although Transit is very precise (accuracies are typically within 0.2 nautical mile), satellites nonetheless pass overhead only intermittently, and navigators using SatNav often must wait an hour or more between fixes. With rocks and other obstacles to avoid, coastal boaters cannot afford to wait such long periods to update their positions. In addition, the higher cost of Transit receivers has placed them beyond the financial reach of many recreational boaters.

The current Federal Radionavigation Plan has scheduled Transit to be taken out of service in 1994. However, the Plan also stipulates a period of overlapping service between Transit and the new GPS system. The launch of GPS satellites may be affected by delays in the space shuttle launch schedule, and the Transit termination date may conceivably be extended somewhat beyond 1994. Whatever the date, until GPS is operational those voyaging beyond the range of Loran-C will find Transit to be the most accurate offshore navigation system available.

GLOBAL POSITIONING SYSTEM (GPS)

The system designed to replace Transit is the eighteen-satellite Global Positioning System (GPS), which will be the first continuously accessible worldwide navigation system.

GPS is designed to provide 24-hour global position-finding capability. The eighteen satellites comprising the system will be placed in higher orbits than those of Transit satellites; since each will remain in view of a ground receiver for a longer period, users will be able to obtain GPS positions at will. The accuracy of GPS, while potentially better than Loran, will not be appreciably better than that available with Transit. Although GPS can provide accuracies as close as 50 feet for military users equipped with special receivers, for reasons of national security accuracy will be intentionally degraded for other users to approximately 300 to 400 feet (the exact figure is still being debated).

Like Loran-C, GPS operates on the basis of time differences, although the procedure is vastly more complicated. A GPS receiver, which contains a sophisticated microcomputer, is programmed with a series of algorithms related to the satellite broadcasts by means of which it is able to synchronize itself with the signals. Once it is "in synch" with a satellite, the receiver can determine an appropriate time difference. Since several satellites will always be in view, the vessel will simultaneously be on several spheres of position; where the spheres intersect is the boat's position.

GPS will provide latitude and longitude position data as well as altitude (for aircraft), velocity, and atomic standard time information. GPS is feasible for automobile navigation as well.

Seven GPS satellites are already in orbit. Although the system was originally scheduled to become operational in 1988, this was before the Challenger shuttle disaster. Present delays in the NASA launch schedule, coupled with the higher priority placed on the launch of several other military satellites, make a later date for full operational status of GPS almost certain. Even then, it's doubtful that the majority of commercial and recreational boaters will rush to purchase GPS receivers; the cost of these units is presently greater than $10,000 and will probably remain quite high for the foreseeable future. Therefore, the acceptance of GPS for coastal navigation by the boating public may be slow.

FUTURE TRENDS

The future holds the promise of still more from the wonderland of satellite navigation. In addition to the two military satellite systems, Transit and GPS, several commercial satellite services—offering both navigational and communication capabilities—are presently under development. Among these, the closest to fruition is Geostar, a system consisting of geosynchronous satellites, handheld transceivers, and a computer ground facility. With Geostar, navigational data approaching GPS accuracy (that won't be degraded at the whim of the Defense Department) will be available, as well as communication capability from the user to any other Geostar transceiver or land telephone. The eventual cost of a Geostar transceiver is expected to be roughly equivalent to that of a present-day Loran receiver, and a monthly subscription fee will be assessed. Geostar expects to be operational in 1989.

As a result of the continued interest in Loran as a navigational tool, the efforts currently being made to improve the system, and its cost-effectiveness for small commercial and recreational users compared to Transit and GPS, there is ample reason to believe that Loran will continue to be a most useful navigational system for years to come.

Appendix A | Loran-C Coverage Area Charts and Data Sheets

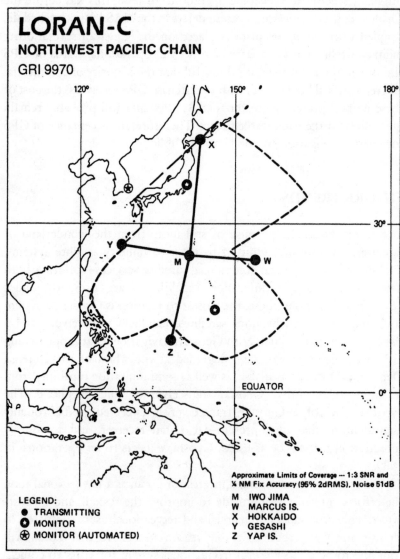

LORAN-C
NORTHWEST PACIFIC CHAIN
GRI 9970

Approximate Limits of Coverage --- 1:3 SNR and ¼ NM Fix Accuracy (95% 2dRMS), Noise 51dB

LEGEND:
- TRANSMITTING
- MONITOR
- MONITOR (AUTOMATED)

M   IWO JIMA
W   MARCUS IS.
X   HOKKAIDO
Y   GESASHI
Z   YAP IS.

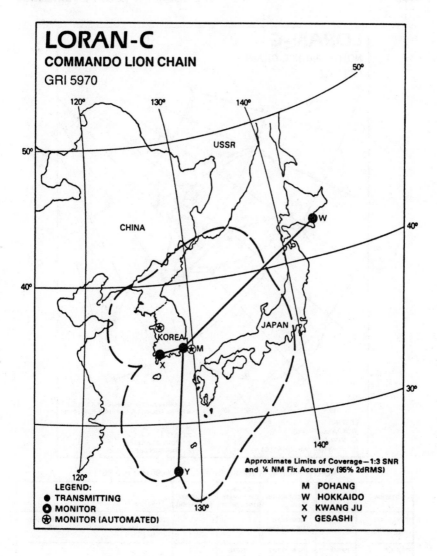

LORAN-C
COMMANDO LION CHAIN
GRI 5970

LEGEND:
● TRANSMITTING
◉ MONITOR
✪ MONITOR (AUTOMATED)

M POHANG
W HOKKAIDO
X KWANG JU
Y GESASHI

Approximate Limits of Coverage—1:3 SNR
and ¼ NM Fix Accuracy (95% 2dRMS)

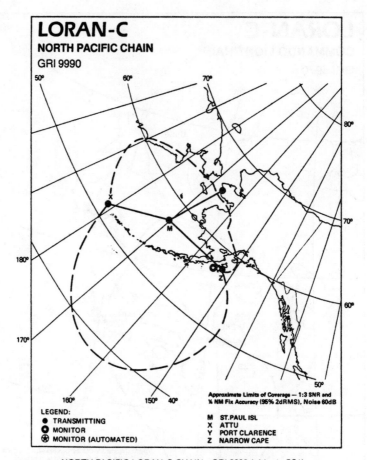

LORAN-C
NORTH PACIFIC CHAIN
GRI 9990

Approximate Limits of Coverage — 1:3 SNR and ¼ NM Fix Accuracy (95% 2dRMS), Noise 60dB

LEGEND:
- ● TRANSMITTING
- ◉ MONITOR
- ⊕ MONITOR (AUTOMATED)

M	ST. PAUL ISL
X	ATTU
Y	PORT CLARENCE
Z	NARROW CAPE

NORTH PACIFIC LORAN-C CHAIN - GRI 9990 (old rate SS1)

STATION	FUNCTION	COORDINATES	CODING DELAY/BASE-LINE LENGTH	RADIATED POWER (KW)	REMARKS
ST. PAUL, AK	MASTER	57 09 12.3 N 170 15 06.8 W		325	CONTROLS X AND Y. EXERCISES OPERATIONAL CONTROL OF CHAIN. TWO PULSE COMMS INSTALLED.
ATTU, AK	XRAY	52 49 44.0 N 173 10 49.0 E	11000/ 3875.25	325	
PORT CLARENCE, AK	YANKEE	65 14 40.3 N 168 53 12.6 W	29000/ 3068.95	1000	
NARROW CAPE, AK	ZULU	57 26 20.2 N 152 22 11.3 W	43000/ 3590.45	400	TWO PULSE COMMS INSTALLED. DUAL-RATED TO GULF OF ALASKA CHAIN.
KODIAK, AK	MONITOR/ CONTROL	57 49 24.3 N 152 19 42.0 W			CONTROL FOR Z.
ADAK, AK	MONITOR	51 53 30.0 N 176 37 42.0 W			
ST. PAUL, AK	MONITOR	57 14 24.0 N 170 06 30.0 W			

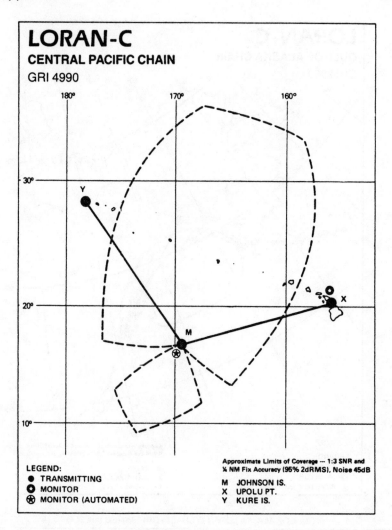

LORAN-C
CENTRAL PACIFIC CHAIN
GRI 4990

LEGEND:
- ● TRANSMITTING
- ◉ MONITOR
- ⊛ MONITOR (AUTOMATED)

Approximate Limits of Coverage — 1:3 SNR and ¼ NM Fix Accuracy (95% 2dRMS), Noise 45dB

M   JOHNSON IS.
X   UPOLU PT.
Y   KURE IS.

CENTRAL PACIFIC LORAN-C CHAIN - GRI 4990 (old rate S1)

STATION	FUNCTION	COORDINATES	CODING DELAY/BASE-LINE LENGTH	RADIATED POWER (KW)	REMARKS
JOHNSTON IS., HI	MASTER	16 44 44.0 N 169 30 31.2 W		325	
UPOLO PT., HI	XRAY	20 14 49.2 N 155 53 09.7 W	11000/ 4972.23	325 325	TIME SERVICE MONITOR
KURE IS., HI	YANKEE	28 23 41.8 N 178 17 30.2 W	29000/ 5253.18	325	
LORMONSITE JOHNSTON IS., HI	MONITOR	16 43 19.5 N 169 32 36.8 W			

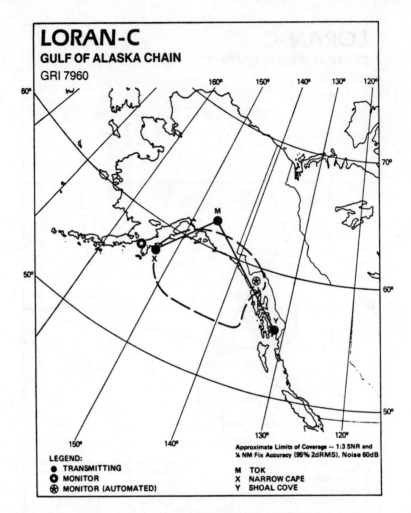

LORAN-C
GULF OF ALASKA CHAIN
GRI 7960

LEGEND:
- ● TRANSMITTING
- ◉ MONITOR
- ✪ MONITOR (AUTOMATED)

M   TOK
X   NARROW CAPE
Y   SHOAL COVE

Approximate Limits of Coverage — 1:3 SNR and ¼ NM Fix Accuracy (95% 2dRMS), Noise 60dB

GULF OF ALASKA LORAN-C CHAIN - GRI 7960 (old rate SL4)

STATION	FUNCTION	COORDINATES	CODING DELAY/BASE-LINE LENGTH	RADIATED POWER (KW)	REMARKS
TOK, AK	MASTER	63 19 42.8 N 142 48 31.9 W		540	TWO PULSE COMMS INSTALLED.
NARROW CAPE, KODIAK IS, AK	XRAY	57 26 20.2 N 152 22 11.3 W	11000/ 2804.45	400	TWO PULSE COMMS INSTALLED. DUAL-RATED TO NORTH PACIFIC CHAIN.
SHOAL COVE, AK	YANKEE	55 26 20.9 N 131 15 19.6 W	26000/ 3851.14	540	TWO PULSE COMMS INSTALLED. DUAL-RATED TO CANADIAN WEST COAST CHAIN.
KODIAK, AK	MONITOR/ CONTROL	57 49 24.3 N 152 19 42.0 W			EXERCISES OPERATIONAL CONTROL OF CHAIN, CONTROL FOR X AND Y.
JUNEAU, AK	MONITOR	58 17 54.8 N 134 24 45.4 W			UNMANNED RECEIVER SITE.

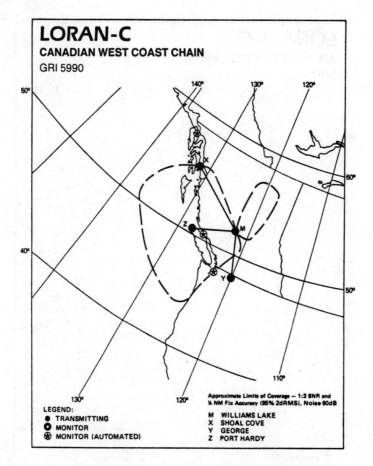

LORAN-C
CANADIAN WEST COAST CHAIN
GRI 5990

LEGEND:
- ● TRANSMITTING
- ◉ MONITOR
- ✪ MONITOR (AUTOMATED)

M WILLIAMS LAKE
X SHOAL COVE
Y GEORGE
Z PORT HARDY

Approximate Limits of Coverage — 1:3 SNR and ¼ NM Fix Accuracy (95% 2dRMS), Noise 60dB

CANADIAN WEST COAST LORAN-C CHAIN - GRI 5990 (old rate SH1)

STATION	FUNCTION	COORDINATES	CODING DELAY/BASE-LINE LENGTH	RADIATED POWER (KW)	REMARKS
WILLIAMS LAKE, BC, CANADA	MASTER	51 57 58.8 N 122 22 02.2 W		400	CONTROL FOR X AND Y. TWO PULSE COMMS INSTALLED
SHOAL COVE, AK	XRAY	55 26 20.9 N 131 15 19.7 W	11000/ 2343.60	540	TWO PULSE COMMS INSTALLED. DUAL-RATED TO GULF OF ALASKA CHAIN.
GEORGE, WA	YANKEE	47 03 48.0 N 119 44 39.5 W	27000/ 1927.36	1600	TWO PULSE COMMS INSTALLED. DUAL-RATED TO U.S. WEST COAST CHAIN.
PORT HARDY, BC, CANADA	ZULU	50 36 29.7 N 127 21 29.4 W	41000/ 1266.61	400	
ALERT BAY, CANADA	MONITOR	50 34 56.0 N 126 54 30.6 W			UNMANNED RECEIVER SITE
WHIDBEY IS, WA	MONITOR	48 17 38.5 N 122 33 59.5 W			UNMANNED RECEIVER SITE
SAND SPIT BC, CANADA	MONITOR	55 14 00.0 N 131 48 50.0 W			UNMANNED RECEIVER SITE

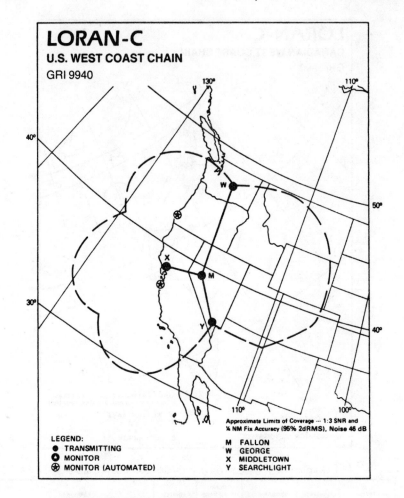

LORAN-C
U.S. WEST COAST CHAIN
GRI 9940

Approximate Limits of Coverage ··· 1:3 SNR and ¼ NM Fix Accuracy (95% 2dRMS), Noise 46 dB

LEGEND:
- ● TRANSMITTING
- ◎ MONITOR
- ✪ MONITOR (AUTOMATED)

- M   FALLON
- W   GEORGE
- X   MIDDLETOWN
- Y   SEARCHLIGHT

U.S. WEST COAST LORAN-C CHAIN - GRI 9940 (old rate SS6)

STATION	FUNCTION	COORDINATES	CODING DELAY/BASE-LINE LENGTH	RADIATED POWER (KW)	REMARKS
FALLON, NV	MASTER	39 33 06.6 N 118 49 56.4 W		400	TWO PULSE COMMS INSTALLED.
GEORGE, WA	WHISKY	47 03 48.0 N 119 44 39.5 W	11000/ 2796.90	1600	TWO PULSE COMMS INSTALLED DUAL RATED TO WEST COAST CANADA CHAIN
MIDDLETOWN, CA	XRAY	38 46 57 0 N 122 29 44.5 W	27000/ 1094.50	400	EXERCISES OPERATIONAL CONTROL OF CHAIN Y TWO PULSE COMMS INSTALLED
SEARCHLIGHT, NV	YANKEE	35 19 18.2 N 114 48 17.4 W	40000/ 1967.30	540	
NORTH BEND, OR	MONSITE	43 24 36.2 N 124 14 27.9 W			UNMANNED RECEIVER SITE
PT PINOS, CA	MONSITE	36 37 59 0 N 121 56 05.6 W			UNMANNED RECEIVER SITE.

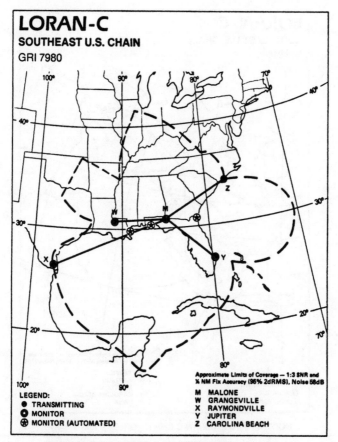

LORAN-C
SOUTHEAST U.S. CHAIN
GRI 7980

LEGEND:
- ● TRANSMITTING
- ◎ MONITOR
- ⊕ MONITOR (AUTOMATED)

Approximate Limits of Coverage — 1:3 SNR and
¼ NM Fix Accuracy (95% 2dRMS), Noise 58dB

M   MALONE
W   GRANGEVILLE
X   RAYMONDVILLE
Y   JUPITER
Z   CAROLINA BEACH

SOUTHEAST U.S. LORAN-C CHAIN - GRI 7980 (old rate SL2)

STATION	FUNCTION	COORDINATES	CODING DELAY/BASE-LINE LENGTH	RADIATED POWER (KW)	REMARKS
MALONE, FL	MASTER	30 59 38.7 N 85 10 09.3 W		800	CONTROL FOR W,X,Y AND Z DUAL-RATED TO GREAT LAKES CHAIN
GRANGEVILLE, LA	WHISKY	30 43 33.0 N 90 49 43.6 W	11000/ 1809 54	800	
RAYMONDVILLE, TX	XRAY	26 31 55.0 N 97 50 00.1 W	23000/ 4443.38	400	
JUPITER, FL	YANKEE	27 01 58.4 N 80 06 53.4 W	4300/ 2201.89	325	
CAROLINA BEACH, NC	ZULU	34 03 46.1 N 77 54 46.7 W	59000/ 2542.73	550	
MAYPORT, FL	MONITOR	30 22 58.9 N 81 25 13.1 W			UNMANNED RECEIVER SITE.
DESTIN, FL	MONITOR	30 28 58.0 N 86 32 32.0 W			UNMANNED RECEIVER SITE.
NEW ORLEANS, LA	MONITOR	29 49 17.3 N 90 01 44.2 W			UNMANNED RECEIVER SITE.

LORAN-C
NORTHEAST U.S. CHAIN
GRI 9960

Approximate Limits of Coverage — 1:3 SNR and ¼ NM Fix Accuracy (95% 2dRMS), Noise 56dB

LEGEND:
● TRANSMITTING
◑ MONITOR
⊕ MONITOR (AUTOMATED)

M SENECA
W CARIBOU
X NANTUCKET
Y CAROLINA BEACH
Z DANA

NORTHEAST U.S. LORAN-C CHAIN - GRI 9960 (old rate S54)

STATION	FUNCTION	COORDINATES	CODING DELAY/BASE-LINE LENGTH	RADIATED POWER (KW)	REMARKS
SENECA, NY	MASTER	42 42 50.6 N 76 49 33.9 W		800	CONTROL FOR W, X, Y AND Z.
CARIBOU, ME	WHISKY	46 48 27.2 N 67 55 37.7 W	11000/ 2797.20	350	
NANTUCKET, MA	XRAY	41 15 11.9 N 69 58 39.1 W	25000/ 1969.93	325	
CAROLINA BEACH, NC	YANKEE	34 03 46.1 N 77 54 46.7 W	39000/ 3221.64	550	
DANA, IN	ZULU	39 51 07.5 N 87 29 12.1 W	54000/ 3162.08	400	
EECEN, WILD-WOOD, NJ	TANGO	38 56 58.2 N 74 52 01.6 W	81500.49	VARIOUS	EXPERIMENTAL STATION, NOT TO BE USED FOR NAVIGATION.
CAPE ELIZABETH, ME	MONITOR	43 33 54.8 N 70 11 58.5 W			UNMANNED RECEIVER SITE.
SANDY HOOK, NJ	MONITOR	40 28 17.0 N 74 01 03.7 W			UNMANNED RECEIVER SITE.
PLUMBROOK, OH	MONITOR	41 22 47.0 N 82 39 38.5 W			UNMANNED RECEIVER SITE.
DUNBAR FOREST, MI	MONITOR	46 23 18.0 N 84 11 06.0 W			UNMANNED RECEIVER SITE

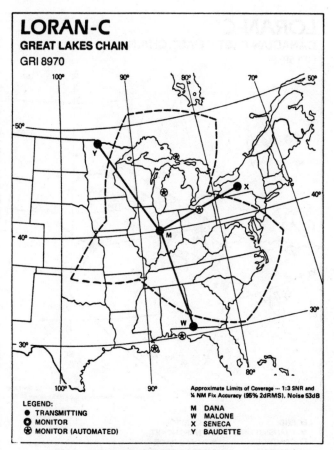

LORAN-C
GREAT LAKES CHAIN
GRI 8970

LEGEND:
- ● TRANSMITTING
- ◎ MONITOR
- ⊛ MONITOR (AUTOMATED)

M DANA
W MALONE
X SENECA
Y BAUDETTE

Approximate Limits of Coverage --- 1:3 SNR and ¼ NM Fix Accuracy (95% 2dRMS), Noise 53dB

GREAT LAKES LORAN-C CHAIN - GRI 8970 (no old rate)

STATION	FUNCTION	COORDINATES	CODING DELAY/BASE-LINE LENGTH	RADIATED POWER (KW)	REMARKS
DANA, IN	MASTER	39 51 07.5 N 87 29 12.1 W		400	DUAL-RATED TO NORTHEAST U.S. CHAIN
MALONE, FL	WHISKY	30 59 38.7 N 85 10 09.3 W	11000/ 3355.11	800	DUAL RATED TO SOUTHEAST U.S. CHAIN.
SENECA, NY	XRAY	42 42 50.6 N 76 49 33.9 W	28000/ 3162.06	800	DUAL RATED TO NORTHEAST U.S. CHAIN. EXERCISES OPERATIONAL CONTROL OF CHAIN.
BAUDETTE, MN	YANKEE	48 36 49.8 N 94 33 18.5 W	44000/ 3753.74	500	
EECEN WILD-WOOD, NJ	TANGO	38 56 58.2 N 74 52 01.6 W	72000/ 1617.92	VARIOUS	EXPERIMENTAL STATION, NOT TO BE USED FOR NAVIGATION.
DUNBAR FOREST	MONITOR	46 23 18.0 N 84 11 06.0 W			
PLUMBROOK, OH	MONITOR	44 22 47.0 N 82 39 38.5 W			UNMANNED RECEIVER SITE.
DESTIN, FL	MONITOR	30 28 58.0 N 86 32 32.0 W			UNMANNED RECEIVER SITE.
NEW ORLEANS, LA	MONITOR	29 49 17.3 N 90 01 44.2 W			UNMANNED RECEIVER SITE.

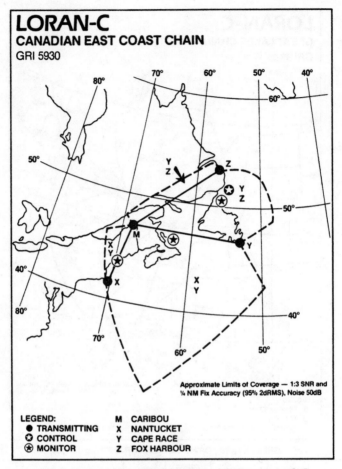

LORAN-C
CANADIAN EAST COAST CHAIN
GRI 5930

Approximate Limits of Coverage — 1:3 SNR and
¼ NM Fix Accuracy (95% 2dRMS), Noise 50dB

LEGEND:
● TRANSMITTING   M CARIBOU
X CONTROL   X NANTUCKET
⊙ CONTROL   Y CAPE RACE
⊛ MONITOR   Z FOX HARBOUR

CANADIAN EAST COST LORAN-C CHAIN - GRI 5930 (old rate SH7)

STATION	FUNCTION	COORDINATES	CODING DELAY/BASE-LINE LENGTH	RADIATED POWER (KW)	REMARKS
CARIBOU, ME	MASTER	46 48 27.2 N 67 55 37.7 W		350	DUAL-RATED TO NORTHEAST U.S. CHAIN
NANTUCKET, MA	XRAY	41 15 11.9 N 69 58 39.1 W	11000/ 2131.88	325	DUAL-RATED TO NORTHEAST U.S. CHAIN
CAPE RACE, NFLD	YANKEE	46 46 32.2 N 53 10 28.2 W	25000/ 3755.02	1500	DUAL-RATED TO NORTH ATLANTIC CHAIN
FOX HARBOR, LAB.	ZULU	52 22 35.2 N 55 42 28.4W	3800/ 3594.59	800	DUAL-RATED TO LABRADOR SEA CHAIN
CAPE ELIZABETH, ME.	MONITOR	43 33 54.8 N 70 11 58.5 W			UNMANNED RECEIVER SITE.
MONTAGUE, P.E.I.	MONITOR	46 11 40.0 N 62 39 37.0 W			UNMANNED RECEIVER SITE.
ST ANTHONY, NFLD	MONITOR/ CONTROL	51 21 37.0 N 55 37 28.0 W			EXERCISES OPERATIONAL CONTROL OF THE CHAIN

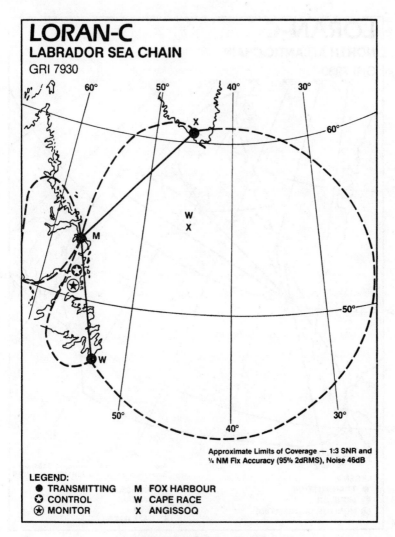

LORAN-C
LABRADOR SEA CHAIN
GRI 7930

Approximate Limits of Coverage — 1:3 SNR and
¼ NM Fix Accuracy (95% 2dRMS), Noise 46dB

LEGEND:
- ● TRANSMITTING   M FOX HARBOUR
- ✪ CONTROL   W CAPE RACE
- ✪ MONITOR   X ANGISSOQ

LABRADOR SEA CHAIN — GRI 7930

STATION	FUNCTION	COORDINATES	CODING DELAY/BASE-LINE LENGTH	RADIATED POWER (KW)	REMARKS
FOX HARBOR LAB.	MASTER	52 22 35.2 N 55 42 28.4 W		800	DUAL-RATED TO CANADIAN EAST COAST CHAIN
CAPE RACE, NFLD	WHISKEY	46 46 32.2 N 53 10 28.2 W	11,000/ 2167.31	1500	DUAL-RATED TO CANADIAN EAST COAST CHAIN
ANDISSOQ, GREENLAND	X-RAY	59 59 17.3 N 45 10 27.5 W	26,000/ 3565.39	760	DUAL-RATED TO NORTH ATLANTIC CHAIN
ST. ANTHONY, NFLD	MONITOR CONTROL	51 21 37.0 N 55 37 28.0 N			EXCERCISES OPTIONAL CONTROL OF CHAIN

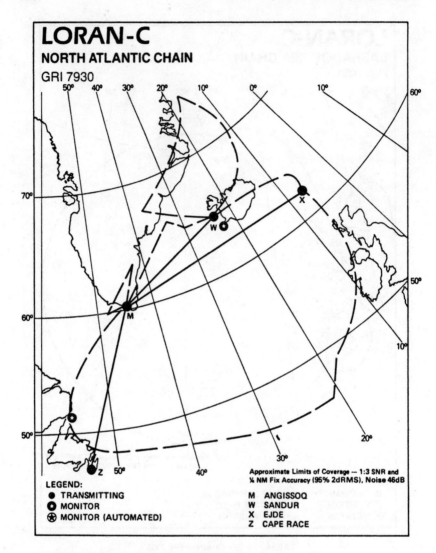

LORAN-C
NORTH ATLANTIC CHAIN
GRI 7930

Approximate Limits of Coverage --- 1:3 SNR and
¼ NM Fix Accuracy (95% 2dRMS), Noise 46dB

LEGEND:
● TRANSMITTING
◉ MONITOR
✪ MONITOR (AUTOMATED)

M ANGISSOQ
W SANDUR
X EJDE
Z CAPE RACE

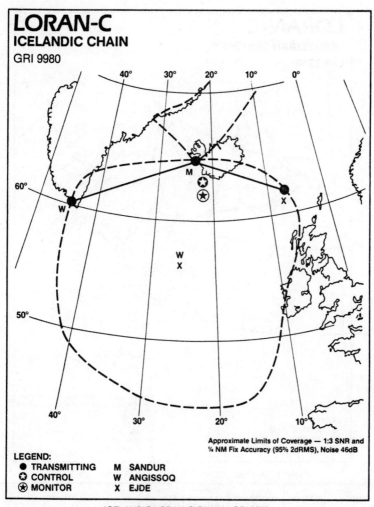

LORAN-C
ICELANDIC CHAIN
GRI 9980

Approximate Limits of Coverage — 1:3 SNR and
¼ NM Fix Accuracy (95% 2dRMS), Noise 46dB

LEGEND:
- ● TRANSMITTING   M   SANDUR
- ✪ CONTROL   W   ANGISSOQ
- ✪ MONITOR   X   EJDE

ICELANDIC LORAN-C CHAIN - GRI 9980

STATION	FUNCTION	COORDINATES	CODING DELAY/BASE-LINE LENGTH	RADIATED POWER (KW)	REMARKS
SANDUR, ICELAND	MASTER	64 54 26.6 N 23 55 21.8 W		1500	HOST NATION MANNED. DUAL-RATED TO NORWEGIAN SEA CHAIN.
ANGISSOQ, GREENLAND	WHISKY	59 59 17.3 N 45 10 27.5 W	11000/ 4068.03	780	HOST NATION MANNED. DUAL-RATED TO LABRADOR SEA CHAIN.
EJDE, FAEROE IS., DENMARK	XRAY	62 17 59.6 N 07 04 26.5 W	30000/ 2944.54	325	
KEFLAVIK, ICELAND	MONITOR/ CONTROL	63 57 23.0 N 22 43 21.0 W			HOST NATION MANNED. EXERCISES OPERATIONAL CONTROL OF CHAIN. CONTROL FOR W AND X.
ST. ANTHONY, NEWFOUNDLAND	MONITOR/ CONTROL	51 21 37.0 N 55 37 28.0 W			HOST NATION MANNED. CONTROL FOR 2.

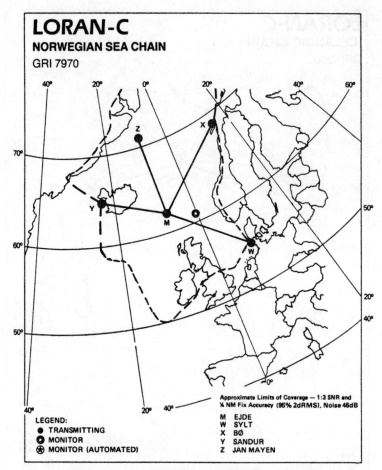

LORAN-C
NORWEGIAN SEA CHAIN
GRI 7970

Approximate Limits of Coverage -- 1:3 SNR and
¼ NM Fix Accuracy (95% 2dRMS), Noise 46dB

LEGEND:
● TRANSMITTING
◉ MONITOR
✹ MONITOR (AUTOMATED)

M EJDE
W SYLT
X BØ
Y SANDUR
Z JAN MAYEN

NORWEGIAN SEA LORAN-C CHAIN - GRI 7970 (old rate SL3)

STATION	FUNCTION	COORDINATES	CODING DELAY/BASE-LINE LENGTH	RADIATED POWER (KW)	REMARKS
EJDE, FAEROE IS. DENMARK	MASTER	62 17 59.6 N 07 04 26.5 W		325	HOST NATION MANNED. DUAL-RATED TO NORTH ATLANTIC CHAIN.
BO, NORWAY	XRAY	68 38 06.2 N 14 27 47.0 E	11000/ 4048.10	165	HOST NATION MANNED.
SYLT, GERMANY	WHISKY	54 48 29.9 N 08 17 36.3 E	26000/ 4065.64	325	
SANDUR, ICELAND	YANKEE	64 54 26.6 N 23 55 21.8 W	˙46000/ 2944.53	1500	HOST NATION MANNED. DUAL-RATED TO NORTH ATLANTIC CHAIN.
JAN MAYEN, NORWAY	ZULU	70 54 52.6 N 08 43 58.7 W	60000/ 3216.30	165	HOST NATION MANNED.
SHETLAND IS., U.K.	MONITOR/ CONTROL	60 26 25.3 N 01 18 05.2 W			CONTROL FOR X,W,Y AND Z.
EJGE, GAEROE IS. DEN.	MONITOR	62 17 59.6 N 07 04 26.5 W			

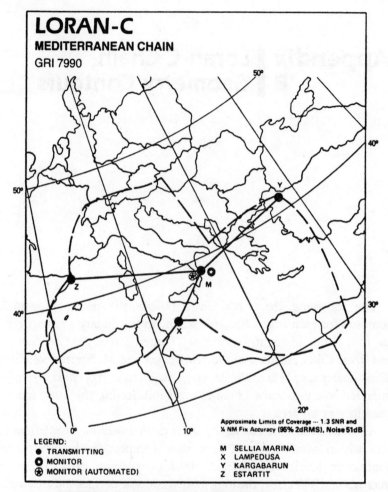

LORAN-C
MEDITERRANEAN CHAIN
GRI 7990

Approximate Limits of Coverage ·· 1:3 SNR and
¼ NM Fix Accuracy (95% 2dRMS). Noise 51dB

LEGEND:
- ● TRANSMITTING
- ◎ MONITOR
- ✪ MONITOR (AUTOMATED)

M   SELLIA MARINA
X   LAMPEDUSA
Y   KARGABARUN
Z   ESTARTIT

MEDITERRANEAN SEA LORAN-C CHAIN - GRI 7990 (old rate SL1)

STATION	FUNCTION	COORDINATES	CODING DELAY/BASE-LINE LENGTH	RADIATED POWER (KW)	REMARKS
SELLIA MARINA, ITALY	MASTER	38 52 20.6 N 16 43 06.2 E		165	
LAMPEDUSA, ITALY	XRAY	35 31 20.8 N 12 31 30.2 E	11000/ 1755.98	325	ATLS STATION.
KARGABARUN, TURKEY	YANKEE	40 58 21.0 N 27 52 01.5 E	29000/ 3273.29	165	
ESTARTIT, SPAIN	ZULU	42 03 36.5 N 03 12 15.5 E	47000/ 3999.74	165	
SELLIA MARINA, ITALY	MONITOR	38 52 20.6 N 16 43 06.2 E			
CROTONE, ITALY	MONITOR	39 00 17.1 N 17 04 48.8 E			

Appendix | Loran-C Chain
B | Geometry Contours

The following charts contain 2 DRMS (95 percent) geometry contours for each triad of master/secondary/secondary transmitters of the four chains within the continental United States, the Canadian East and West Coast chains, and the Norwegian and Mediterranean chains. These charts supplement the coverage diagrams in Appendix A, and are intended solely to assist Loran-C users in selecting the most accurate triad in a given area.

As indicated on the charts, the short dashed contour line defines the area within which Loran-C users should expect (with a 95 percent confidence level) to obtain a 500-foot position error for a 0.1 microsecond TD error; the long dashed contour defines the area within which 1,000-foot position errors for a 0.1 ms TD error are obtained; the solid contour line defines a 1,500-foot position error for a 0.1 ms TD error. These contours are based solely on the geometry of the various transmitters within the applicable triad, and do not include the range limits of Loran-C coverage.

The diagrams are abstracted from the U.S. Coast Guard publication, "Specification of the Transmitted Loran-C Signal," COMDTINST M16562.4.

LORAN-C
U.S. WEST COAST CHAIN
GRI 9940

2 drms fix accuracy; $\sigma = 0.1$ μs

.... 500 ft.

— — — 1000 ft.

———————— 1500 ft.

Note: These contours are based on geometry only and do **not** include range limits.

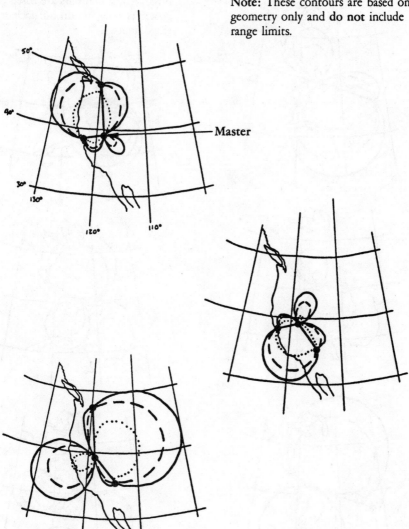

LORAN-C
SOUTHEAST U.S. CHAIN
GRI 7980

2 drms fix accuracy; $\sigma = 0.1$ μs

.... 500 ft.

—— —— —— 1000 ft.

——————————— 1500 ft.

Note: These contours are based on geometry only and **do not** include range limits.

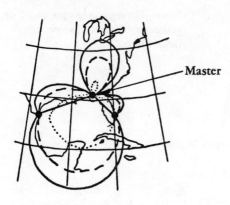

Master

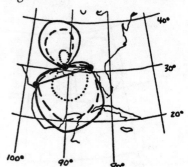

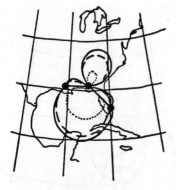

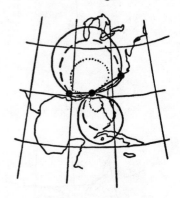

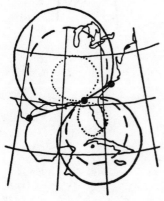

LORAN-C
NORTHEAST U.S. CHAIN
GRI 9960

2 drms fix accuracy; $\sigma = 0.1$ μs

····························	500 ft.
— — —	1000 ft.
————————	1500 ft.

Note: These contours are based on geometry only and **do not** include range limits.

Master

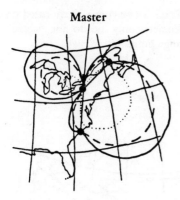

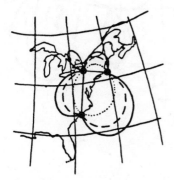

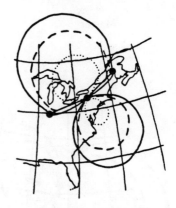

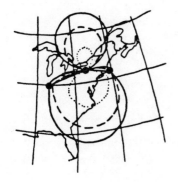

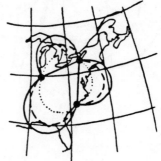

LORAN-C
GREAT LAKES CHAIN
GRI 8970

2 drms fix accuracy; $\sigma = 0.1\ \mu s$

····························	500 ft.
—— —— ——	1000 ft.
——————————	1500 ft.

Note: These contours are based on geometry only and **do not** include range limits.

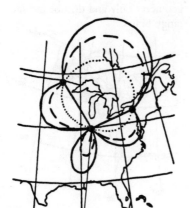

Master

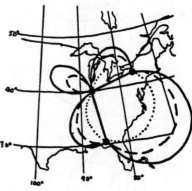

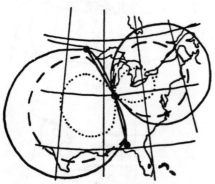

LORAN-C
CANADIAN WEST COAST CHAIN
GRI 5990

2 drms fix accuracy; $\sigma = 0.1$ μs

································ 500 ft.

—— —— —— 1000 ft.

———————— 1500 ft.

Note: These contours are based on geometry only and **do not** include range limits.

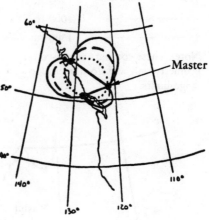

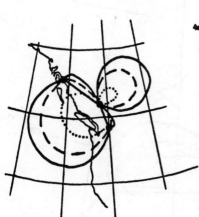

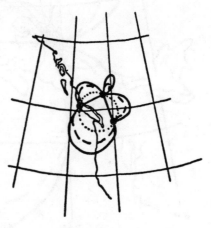

LORAN-C
CANADIAN EAST COAST CHAIN
GRI 5930

2 drms fix accuracy; $\sigma = 0.1$ μs

....   500 ft.

—— —— ——   1000 ft.

————————   1500 ft.

Note: These contours are based on geometry only and **do not** include range limits.

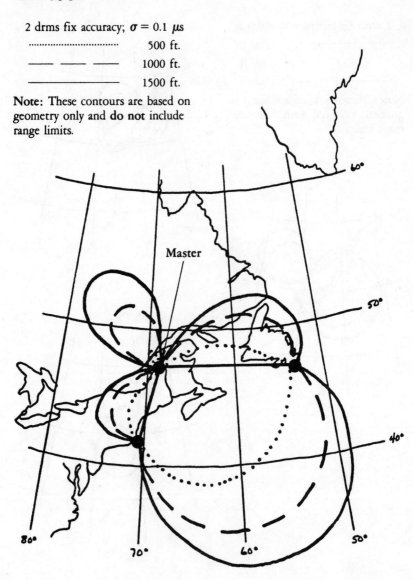

LORAN-C
NORWEGIAN SEA CHAIN
GRI 7970

2 drms fix accuracy; $\sigma = 0.1$ μs

....	500 ft.
—— —— ——	1000 ft.
——————————	1500 ft.

Note: These contours are based on geometry only and **do not** include range limits.

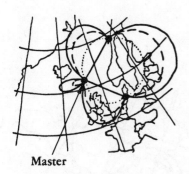

Master

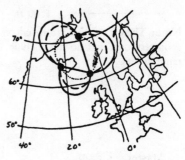

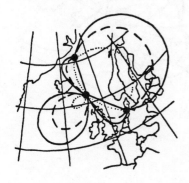

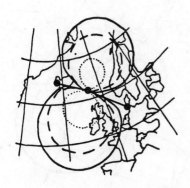

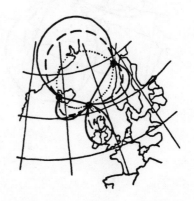

LORAN-C
MEDITERRANEAN CHAIN
GRI 7990

2 drms fix accuracy; $\sigma = 0.1\ \mu s$

....   500 ft.

———— ——— ————   1000 ft.

————————————————   1500 ft.

Note: These contours are based on geometry only and **do not** include range limits.

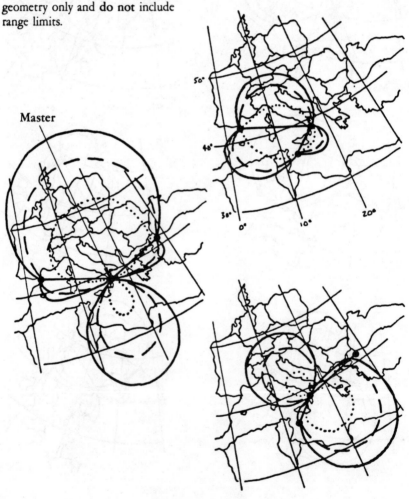

Master

Appendix C | Known Sources of Radio Frequency Interference

The following tables pinpoint the locations, frequencies, and nominal transmission powers of known sources of radio frequency interference within the 70 to 115 kHz frequency band along the East Coast of the United States and Canada and within the 70 to 150 kHz frequency band along the West Coast of the United States and Canada, in Hawaii, and in Alaska. To optimize Loran-C reception when operating in close proximity to some or all of these transmitters, notch filtering may be required to suppress RF noise.

LORAN-C INTERFERENCE LIST—70-150 kHz WESTERN REGION

FREQUENCY	TRANSMITTER LOCATION (source of interference)	AUTHORIZED POWER (kW)	OBSERVED FIELD STRENGTH (dB/uV/m)				
			Point Pinos CA	North Bend OR	Comox BC	Juneau AK	Kodiak AK
119.85	San Francisco	50	75.0		55.0	34.3	60.4
123.0	Nanaimu BC	3		38.4	80.8	36.1	
128.25	San Diego	—			43.0	36.9	
128.95	Honolulu	—		34.0			
133.15	Vancouver	25		49.1	83.9	40.2	
148.2	San Francisco	50					
148.2	San Diego	50	43.5				

LORAN-C INTERFERENCE LIST—70-115 kHz EASTERN REGION

FREQUENCY	TRANSMITTER LOCATION (source of interference)	AUTHORIZED POWER (kW)	FREQUENCY	TRANSMITTER LOCATION (source of interference)	AUTHORIZED POWER (kW)
70.387	Newfoundland	1.2	116.8	—	—
71.142	Nova Scotia	2.7	117.157	Quebec	1.2
71.437	Quebec	1.2	119.85	Norfolk	2.0
73.6	Nova Scotia	250	125.8	Manitoba	10
76.4	—	—	128.25	New York	—
77.5	—	—	128.25	Newport, RI	—
84.465	Newfoundland	1.2	128.25	Honolulu	—
84.73	Ontario	0.9	131.1	Ontario	3.0
85.37	Nova Scotia	2.4	133.15	Halifax	15
85.43	Nova Scotia	2.4	134.9	Annapolis	100
88.0	Annapolis	50	137.7	—	—
(±85)	—	—	139.8	Newport, RI	20
112.3	Ontario	3.0	(±85)	—	—
112.5	Halifax	15.0	139.8	Norfolk	100
113.2	Ottawa	3.0	(±85)	—	—
113.827	Nova Scotia	2.4	143.6	Nova Scotia	40
114.3	Quebec	1.2	145.4	—	—
115.3	Halifax	250	148.5	Ontario	3.0
116.0	—	—			

Appendix D | Loran-C Chart Agencies

Loran-C overprinted charts are an integral part of the overall Loran-C system. To obtain optimum accuracy from Loran-C, users are urged to purchase up-to-date Loran charts of their operating areas. Charts may be ordered from the following government agencies.

U.S. CHARTS

Distribution Division (OA/C44)
National Ocean Survey
Riverdale, Maryland 20840
Telephone: (301) 436-6990

These charts and chart catalogs are also available from many local authorized agents, ship's stores, and chandleries.

CANADIAN CHARTS

The Canadian Hydrographic Services issues charts and chart catalogs for the Canadian East and West coasts and for the Great Lakes.

Canadian Hydrographic Services
Department of Fisheries and Environment
Ottawa, Ontario K1A 0E6 Canada

NON-U.S. AND CANADIAN CHARTS

Charts of areas of the world other than the United States and Canada may be ordered from:

The Defense Mapping Agency (DMA)
Topographic Center, Attn. DDCP
6500 Brookes Lane
Washington, D.C. 20315

Mariners are cautioned also to keep informed of changes in aids to navigation, including those related to the operational status of Loran-C transmitters, as detailed in the local *Notice to Mariners*, printed weekly by the Coast Guard and mailed free to interested mariners. Contact your local Coast Guard district office to add your name to the subscription list.

Appendix E | Glossary

Absolute (navigational) accuracy. A measure of your Loran-C receiver's ability to determine your true geographic position. See also *Repeatable accuracy.*

Acquisition. The reception and identification of Loran-C signals from the selected master and secondaries with sufficient reliability to allow subsequent tracking.

Additional secondary factors (ASF). Land path factors, essentially variations in the conductivity of the earth's surface, which cause Loran-C signals to travel more slowly over a landmass than over seawater. The degree of retardation varies with the terrain and the type and concentration of ground cover, and cannot be predicted. Local ASFs must therefore be determined empirically. ASFs degrade absolute accuracy but have minimal effect on repeatable accuracy.

Ambiguity. Uncertainty about your actual position brought about when two Loran-C LOPs cross at two local points rather than in a single location. In extreme cases, selecting the proper fix becomes difficult, perhaps requiring supplemental input from radio-direction finding, dead reckoning, or another navigational aid.

Antenna. Any device that converts incoming electromagnetic waves to electrical signals.

Antenna coupler. A preamplifier on which the Loran-C antenna is mounted. It boosts the low power of an incoming signal to the strength and impedance necessary at the receiver.

Baseline. The segment of a great circle that joins the master transmitter and a secondary station. The most accurate Loran readings are obtained on or near the baseline.

Baseline extension. The extension of the baseline beyond the two stations it joins. Loran readings in the vicinity of the baseline extension are much less accurate than those obtained near the baseline, and can lead to a position ambiguity.

Blink. A warning to the Loran receiver that technical problems exist in the system. The warning comes from a secondary transmitter in the first two pulses of the secondary pulse group, and the receiver then notifies the operator by a light or flashing numbers that the data are in error. If the problem is in the secondary, switching to a new secondary may enable resumed use of the chain. If the problem is in the master, the chain itself cannot be used.

Carrier frequency. The assigned frequency of a radio transmitter, although the actual transmission frequency at any time may be somewhat higher or lower. The carrier frequency of Loran-C radio signals is 100 kHz.

Chain. A network of Loran-C transmitters consisting of a master and two or more secondaries. Each chain identifies itself by means of its characteristic group repetition interval (GRI).

Coding delay. The interval between the time a secondary receives the signal from the master and the time it sends its own signal. Also called the *secondary coding delay.*

Crossing angle. The angle, from 0 to 90 degrees, at which two LOPs cross one another, creating a fix.

Cross-rate/cross-chain interference. Radio interference in the reception of signals from one Loran-C chain caused by the transmissions of stations in another chain.

Cross track error. The distance of a vessel to port or starboard of its intended courseline.

Cycle slip. The failure of a Loran receiver to lock onto and sample an incoming signal at the normal 30-microsecond sampling point. Rather, the receiver locks on 10 ms earlier or later, or at multiples of 10 ms intervals. Time difference readings will be in error by a similar amount, which will result in position errors.

Differential gain. Indicates the maximum difference in signal strengths between the transmissions of a master and a secondary station that the receiver is capable of processing properly. A high differential gain is desirable, indicating that the receiver can successfully compare a very strong signal with a very weak one. High differential gain is particularly important when operating near a transmitter.

Dual-rated station. A Loran-C transmitting station that is an operational part of two chains.

Dynamic range. A measure of the ability of a receiver to process both weak and strong signals. *Sensitivity* indicates how far from a station the receiver can function under conditions of low signal strength and high noise. *Dynamic range*, in combination with sensitivity, indicates how close to a station a receiver can function.

ECD. Envelope-to-cycle difference, a measure of Loran signal distortion.

Envelope matching. A technique in which the envelope (the outline of the total radio-frequency cycles comprising a single pulse) is matched to acquire and track a signal. Once used heavily by Loran-A receivers, it is used only for coarse matching in Loran-C.

Fix. A vessel's position, determined by finding the point where two or more lines of position (LOPs) intersect.

Frequency band. The range between the highest and lowest frequencies of a transmission. The Loran-C frequency band is from 90 kHz to 110 kHz, with 100 kHz being the carrier frequency.

Fringe area. The geographic area beyond the normal range of reliable Loran-C coverage where Loran signal strength, although weak, may still be used for navigation. When using Loran in fringe areas, the operator usually must cycle-step the signal, a technique requiring above-average understanding of Loran-C.

GDOP. Geometric dilution of position, a local degradation of position accuracy caused by the geodetic relationship of stations within a chain. The geometry of some secondary pairs is such that crossing angles in certain locations within an area of coverage are very shallow, resulting in inaccurate fixes.

Geodetic accuracy. A measure of the accuracy of a vessel's geographic position as indicated by a Loran-C fix. Absolute accuracy.

Gradient. The spacing between adjacent Loran LOPs as determined by the number of nautical miles of separation represented by each microsecond of time difference (TD). Gradient varies with a vessel's position within the Loran-C coverage area, becoming greater the farther the vessel is from a secondary transmitter. Large gradients cause correspondingly larger position errors for every 0.1 microsecond of receiver readout or user interpolation error.

Ground. An electrically neutral point on a vessel that provides a Loran receiver with direct electrical access to the "earth."

Groundwave. The part of a transmitted radio signal that follows the curve of the earth's surface and remains near the ground. Since it travels the most direct path to a vessel, the time required for the groundwave to propagate from the transmitter to a vessel is a true measure of the vessel's distance from the transmitter, assuming the signal's velocity remains constant.

Group repetition interval (GRI). The time interval in microseconds between the start of one transmission from the master station in a Loran-C chain and the start of the next. Between the two master transmissions, each secondary transmitter in its turn sends its signal, after waiting the period of the secondary coding delay. The GRI also serves to identify the chain.

In-band noise. Any electrical RF interference that occurs within the normal Loran-C frequency band of 90 kHz to 110 kHz.

Ionosphere. A high-altitude layer of the earth's atmosphere that greatly affects the propagation of radio waves. A part of every radio signal travels upward into the atmosphere and bounces off the ionosphere, returning to earth as a skywave. The height of the ionosphere varies between approximately 25 and 250 miles, increasing during the daytime and decreasing at night.

kHz. 1,000 cycles per second of radio frequency oscillation.

Land path variable. A factor used to compensate for the fact that Loran-C signal speeds depend on the kind of terrain traversed—open ocean, flat land, mountains, farmland, desert, cities, etc.

LCD. Liquid crystal display. A display of black numbers or letters on a light background. An LCD is relatively easy to read regardless of light conditions.

LED. Light-emitting diode. A display of red numbers or letters on a black background, often difficult to read in bright outdoor light.

Line of position (LOP). A line composed of an infinite number of points, any one of which represents a possible position for a vessel based on a single navigational observation. In the case of Loran-C, that observation is the time difference (TD) between the arrivals of the master signal and the signal from a secondary. The LOP is the locus of all points within the coverage area exhibiting that same time difference. The vessel's position is somewhere on the LOP. Two intersecting LOPs are required for a position fix. See also *Loran-C LOP*.

Loran-C LOP. A line printed on a NOAA Loran-C overprinted chart that represents a constant time difference and thus a constant difference in distance from two transmitting stations in a chain. The Loran receiver of a vessel located anywhere along the LOP would display the same TD.

Loran-C system. A long-range radio navigation system maintained by the U.S. Coast Guard and operating at an assigned carrier frequency of 100 kHz that utilizes pulsed signals from widely separated radio transmitting stations. The differences in arrival times of pulses from two stations are measured, and these time differences are used to determine position relative to the transmitter. The system is intended as an aid to navigation in coastal waters.

Master transmitter. The transmitting station in a Loran-C chain whose signals both identify the chain and provide the reference by which all the secondary stations in that chain synchronize their signals.

Maximum operating range. The maximum distance within the coverage area of a chain at which reception is possible within a specified accuracy and signal-to-noise ratio (SNR).

Microsecond. One-millionth of a second of time.

Minimum operating range. The range, generally about 15 to 20 nautical miles, within which the receiver may not be able to track an incoming Loran-C signal due to cycle slip.

Navigation computer. A microprocessor built into the Loran-C receiver that uses the direction and rate of change in the vessel's position to calculate navigational information such as bearing and range, course, speed, velocity made good, off course and steering indications, estimated time en route and time of arrival, and anchor alerts. It can also create and store waypoints and routes, initiate automatic waypoint sequencing, and interface with the vessel's autopilot.

Notch filters. Fixed (preset) or variable narrow-band radio frequency filters in a Loran-C receiver that filter unwanted transmission interference from RF sources external to a vessel. They will not suppress noise from onboard sources. To be effective, preset notch filters must be calibrated to filter the specific frequency of RF interference encountered in a particular locale.

Phase coding. The predetermined pattern of positive and negative phases in each pulse of Loran-C master and secondary signals. Phase coding helps the receiver distinguish signals transmitted by master and secondary stations, and reduces skywave contamination.

Receiver. An electronic device that processes incoming Loran-C radiowave signals from the antenna coupler and precisely measures the difference in arrival time of a signal from a master transmitter and two secondary transmitters; these time differences (TDs) are displayed on the receiver readout.

Remote readout. A separate Loran-C display that makes steering information provided by the navigation computer available in the wheelhouse or cockpit. Most remote readouts display cross track error (XTE) and a graphic steering display.

Repeatable accuracy. Precision. A measure of the accuracy with which Loran-C is able to guide you back to a location once visited. The time differences (TDs) of the location noted on the previous visit are used to return on subsequent visits. Loran-C repeatable accuracy is as good as 50 feet.

Route. A sequence of intermediate waypoints to which a navigator travels on the way to a final destination. If desired, routes may be stored in memory and recalled for use as needed.

Secondary phase factor. A measure of the change in propagation speed of Loran-C signals as they travel over seawater paths en route to a receiver. Secondary phase factors can be predicted accurately.

Secondary transmitter. One of two to four stations in a Loran-C chain that transmit their signals on cue from the master transmitter. Formerly called "slaves," the secondaries are designed W, X, Y, or Z.

Settle. The process by which a Loran-C receiver aligns itself to the phase codes of incoming signals, locates and tracks at the correct 30-microsecond sampling point, establishes the fact that it is tracking a groundwave, and indicates that time differences are valid. Settling times vary from several minutes after the receiver is switched on when SNRs are strong, to 15 to 20 minutes when signals are weak (as in fringe areas). During the settling time, time differences on the receiver readout will blink.

Signal-to-noise ratio (SNR). The ratio of the strength of Loran-C signals at the 30-microsecond timing point to the strength of background RF interference in the Loran-C frequency band. All Loran-C receivers are capable of tracking signals with SNRs of 1:3 or greater. Loran-C coverage charts show the area within which the SNR exceeds 1:3.

Skywave. The part of a transmitted Loran-C signal that bounces off the ionosphere rather than traveling a direct path over the ground to the receiver. Reception of skywaves rather than groundwaves results in position errors, and because skywaves are often stronger than their companion groundwaves they often cause interference with ground-wave reception.

Time difference (TD). The difference in microseconds between the time a master signal is received by a Loran receiver and the time a secondary signal is received. The resulting TD is displayed on the receiver readout.

Tracking. The process of continually timing incoming signals at the intended 30-microsecond timing point.

Waypoint. A geographic location to which the navigator wishes to travel, defined as the intersection of two Loran LOPs or by latitude/ longitude coordinates. Waypoints may be permanently stored in waypoint memory for later recall, and may be organized into routes.

Waypoint zero. The TDs of the vessel's present position.

Index

214